A BLACKLETTER
STATEMENT OF
FEDERAL
ADMINISTRATIVE
LAW
2ND EDITION

A BLACKLETTER STATEMENT OF FEDERAL ADMINISTRATIVE LAW

2ND EDITION

**Section of Administrative Law
and Regulatory Practice
American Bar Association**

Cover design by Andrea Siegert/ABA Publishing.

The materials contained herein represent the opinions of the authors and/or the editors, and should not be construed to be the views or opinions of the law firms or companies with whom such persons are in partnership with, associated with, or employed by, nor of the American Bar Association or the Section of Administrative Law and Regulatory Practice unless adopted pursuant to the bylaws of the Association.

Nothing contained in this book is to be considered as the rendering of legal advice for specific cases, and readers are responsible for obtaining such advice from their own legal counsel. This book is intended for educational and informational purposes only.

Printed in the United States of America.

21 20 19 8 7 6

Library of Congress Cataloging-in-Publication Data

A blackletter statement of federal administrative law / by the Section of Administrative Law and Regulatory Practice, American Bar Association. — Second edition.
    pages cm
 Includes bibliographical references and index.
 ISBN 978-1-62722-302-7 (alk. paper)
 1. United States. Administrative Procedure Act. 2. Administrative procedure—United States. I. American Bar Association. Section of Administrative Law and Regulatory Practice.
 KF5407.B53 2013
 342.73'06--dc23

2013034067

Discounts are available for books ordered in bulk. Special consideration is given to state bars, CLE programs, and other bar-related organizations. Inquire at Book Publishing, ABA Publishing, American Bar Association, 321 N. Clark Street, Chicago, Illinois 60654-7598.

www.ShopABA.org

TABLE OF CONTENTS

PREFACE

When the American Bar Association's Section of Administrative Law and Regulatory Practice approved the first BLACKLETTER STATEMENT OF FEDERAL ADMINISTRATIVE LAW in late 2001, it declared its "aim[] to [be to] summarize in manageable length and format the basic propositions of current federal administrative law."[1] In an early example of what has subsequently come to be known as crowd-sourcing, the Section enlisted a broad corps of the leading lights in the field to produce a document whose strength, then-Section Chair Ron Levin noted in *his* preface, lies in the way it "encapsulates the *collective* views of a wide segment of administrative lawyers and scholars."[2] As a result, the document's reporters found "irresistible"—as do I—the temptation to hope that others would "find the document worthy of something akin to *Skidmore* deference . . . due to 'the thoroughness evident in its consideration, the validity of its reasoning, its consistency with earlier and later pronouncements, and all those factors which give it power to persuade, if lacking power to control.'"[3] In retrospect, it is safe to say that this confidence was warranted, as evidenced by the dozens of times the document has been cited in the scholarly literature and, more generally, by the respect with which it is held by experts in the field.

The feasibility of this project arose from what the reporters described as the "constitution[al]" quality of the Administrative Procedure Act [APA]—i.e., its centrality and imperviousness to amendment.[4] "At the same time," the reporters noted, the "requirements of administrative law extend far beyond that document, to include the judicial gloss on the APA, other decisions that seem pure examples of federal common law, the Constitution, several other generally applicable

---

1. 54 Admin. L. Rev. 1, 6 (2002).
2. *Id*. at 2 (emphasis in original).
3. *Id*. at 7-8 (quoting Skidmore v. Swift & Co., 323 U.S. 134 (1944)). The chief reporter was Paul Verkuil, assisted by Michael Herz and John Duffy.
4. *Id*. at 7.

statutes, and executive orders."[5] While Congress is once again considering sweeping revisions to the APA, the statute has remained unamended since the first edition of the Blackletter Statement. But courts have continued to interpret and reinterpret the act (and their prior holdings), other laws have been amended, and over 300 more executive orders have been issued.

Completed in the summer of 2001, the text of the Blackletter Statement was exactly a decade old when former assistant reporter Michael Herz became Section Chair in August 2011. Every chair is customarily supposed to have his or her "projects," and Michael's most lasting (and undoubtedly most time-consuming) was to spur the first update of the Statement. When he launched the effort in October 2011, he optimistically set a goal of putting the final draft before the Section Council at its April meeting—and so he did, although it was the April 2013 meeting.

The work turned out to involve more than just updating the document, however. In several areas, the (re)drafters concluded that the Statement crossed its own line from description to prescription and should be more carefully circumscribed. Sections were lengthened, shortened, and relocated to produce a document that is not just current but also more consistent in substance and style and better organized.

Michael was recognized in his previous role for "acting as a virtual chief operating officer for the project, [bearing] the brunt of the responsibility for nudging participants into action, mediating among strong-minded advocates of various positions, keeping the flow of documents moving, and performing numerous other administrative chores that made the life of a Section Chair easier."[6] He did all these things and more again, except this time he *was* the Section Chair for most of the same time.

Ron Levin was the Section Chair whose job was made easier by Michael's prior work. The reporters last time noted Ron's "indispensable role in keeping the group on task, drafting language, and nudging

---

5. *Id.*
6. *Id.* at 3.

those with differing views toward resolution."[7] This time around, Ron continued to play at least a helpful—and in many cases crucial—role with regard to almost every section, and so he also deserves special mention in this respect (as in so many others).

The other contributors are best recognized on a chapter-by-chapter basis:

Adjudication: Michael Asimow was the principal oar-puller, aided by Anne O'Connell, Jack Beermann, Jeff Litwak, Anne Young, and Greg Ogden.

Rulemaking: Jeff Lubbers was the key player here, assisted by Jeff Rosen and Anne O'Connell.

Scope of Review: Richard Murphy and Kathryn Watts were in charge here, with input from Bill Funk, Hal Bruff, and Kevin Stack.

Availability of Review: Richard Murphy and Bill Funk did the lion's share of work here, aided by Kathryn Watts.

FOIA: Bernie Bell took the lead here, helped by Mark Zaid and Jim O'Reilly.

Government Management: Kevin Stack, Anne O'Connell, Bill Funk, and Jeff Lubbers collaborated on the revisions.

Although the foregoing were the key drafters of the revisions, each chapter was laid before the Section Council for approval—as was, ultimately, the document as a whole. The Council made its own changes and corrections, and it is the Council's engaged scrutiny that makes this document truly a publication of and by the Section rather than the individual participants.

---

7.   *Id.* at 12.

The reporters for the original Statement opined that "administrative law is not itself an area of legal specialty."[8] This, too, may be an opinion in need of updating, as more and more of us find ourselves specializing in precisely that field. To the extent that is true, it is in no small measure because the Blackletter Statement, and the other work product of the Section, have helped organize and articulate this slippery body of law with sufficient clarity and felicity that practitioners can effectively function within it.

James W. Conrad, Jr.
Chair

---

8. *Id.* at 6.

A BLACKLETTER STATEMENT OF FEDERAL ADMINISTRATIVE LAW

PREPARED BY THE SECTION OF ADMINISTRATIVE LAW AND
REGULATORY PRACTICE OF THE AMERICAN BAR ASSOCIATION
APPROVED BY THE SECTION COUNCIL, APRIL 14, 2013

CONTENTS

PART ONE
ADJUDICATION

PART ONE
ADJUDICATION

Adjudication is the agency process for issuing an order that resolves particular rights or duties. It would be impracticable to canvass the entire subject of administrative adjudication throughout the range of its uses. The present treatment is bounded in two respects: it deals only with federal administrative law, and it deals only with fundamental elements, as specified by constitutional due process and by the Administrative Procedure Act (APA).

I. DUE PROCESS REQUIREMENTS FOR A HEARING

A. Basic Principles

Due process analysis requires, first, a determination that there exists a constitutionally protected interest within the meaning of the constitutional Due Process Clauses; second, a determination that there has been a "deprivation" of one of those interests; third, a determination of what process is due in order to protect those interests. Due process attaches only to "state action."

B. Protected Interest

Procedural due process requires a "substantive predicate," which is a substantive right to "life, liberty or property." The substantive rights that are protected by due process must be independently determined, apart from the demand for procedural protection itself.

Substantive rights may be derived from a variety of sources. In the case of property, the right or entitlement must be grounded outside the federal Constitution, which presupposes but does not itself create property rights. An entitlement requires the presence of substantive standards that constrain the discretion of governmental decisionmakers.Protected property rights are established by state or federal law, including both statutory and common law. Liberty interests may be based on state or federal law, or on the federal Constitution, including the due process clause itself.

C. Deprivation

To constitute a deprivation for due process purposes, government action must adversely affect a protected interest. Negligent actions, however, even if tortious, do not amount to a deprivation for due process purposes.

D. Process Due

Determining the procedures required by due process involves consideration of three factors: (1) the strength of the private interest, (2) the risk of error and the probable value of additional or substitute procedural safeguards to avoid error, and (3) the strength of the government's interest. These considerations govern both the adequacy and timing of the procedures required. The requirements of due process vary with the particulars of the proceeding. While in some circumstances an individualized adjudicatory hearing is required, in other cases notice of the subjects of the agency proceeding and the opportunity to submit written comments or oral comments at a legislative-type hearing may be sufficient.

E. Legislative-type Determinations

An adjudicatory hearing is not required, as a matter of constitutional due process, when agency action is legislative in character rather than adjudicatory.

II. RIGHT TO A HEARING UNDER THE ADMINISTRATIVE PROCEDURE ACT

A. Formal Hearings under the APA

Subject to the set of exceptions set forth in § 554(a) of the APA and described below in § II.B, a formal hearing is required by the APA in "every case of adjudication required by statute to be determined on the record after opportunity for an agency hearing." Where a federal statute requires such an on-the-record hearing, the hearing must comply with the provisions of §§ 554, 556, and 557 of the APA.

Determining whether a statute that calls for a hearing (but does not use the words "on the record") triggers the formal adjudication requirements of the APA is a matter of statutory interpretation. The prevailing view is that courts will defer to a reasonable agency interpretation that such a statute does not trigger the APA's formal adjudication provisions.

B. Agency Action Excepted from Adjudication Requirements

The APA does not require a formal hearing to the extent that there is involved a matter subject to a subsequent trial de novo in a court; the selection or tenure of an employee; proceedings in which decisions rest solely on inspections, tests, or elections; the conduct of military or foreign-affairs functions; cases in which an agency is acting as an agent for a court; or the certification of worker representatives.

III. PROCEDURAL REQUIREMENTS FOR FORMAL HEARINGS UNDER THE ADMINISTRATIVE PROCEDURE ACT

A. Basic Requirements

Hearings required to be conducted under the APA must follow the procedures required by § 556 of the APA.

B.   Openness

Although § 556 of the APA does not specifically state that hearings must be open, the very concept of a hearing comparable to a judicial proceeding entails norms of openness. Thus, agency hearings generally must be open to the public.

Notwithstanding the general policy favoring open hearings, agencies may close hearings for reasons of confidentiality or to protect potential spectators, witnesses, or parties to a hearing. In such circumstances, the presiding administrative law judge "may take only the most limited action necessary to sufficiently protect the interest perceived to be paramount to the interest of the public in an open hearing."

C.   Burden of Proof

Section 556(d) requires that, unless another statute provides authority for a different allocation for the burden of proof, the burden of proof with respect to any decision rests with the proponent of that decision. For purposes of § 556(d), the term "burden of proof" means the burden of persuasion. Unless a statute or rule specifies otherwise, the standard of proof in agency adjudication is the familiar "preponderance of the evidence" standard.

D.   Rules of Evidence

The APA requires that formal adjudicatory decisions be "supported by and in accordance with the reliable, probative, and substantial evidence." Agency adjudications need not conform to the Federal Rules of Evidence, and agency adjudicators may consider evidence, such as hearsay, that would be inadmissible in federal courts. Such evidence may form the sole basis for agency decisions. Under § 556 of the APA, agency adjudicators must "provide for the exclusion of irrelevant, immaterial, or unduly repetitious evidence." Subject to that requirement, agencies have power to prescribe their own rules of evidence, provided that those rules are consistent with constitutional standards of due process.

Though agency adjudications are not governed by the Federal Rules of Evidence as a general matter, the attorney-client privilege and like privileges may be asserted in an agency proceeding. Agencies may take official notice of facts not supported by record evidence. Where an agency has taken official notice of a material fact, parties to the proceeding are entitled to an opportunity to demonstrate the contrary.

E.   Oral Evidence and Cross-Examination

Parties to formal adjudications are entitled under § 556(d) of the APA to present their case or their defense "by oral or documentary evidence." The right to present oral evidence does not apply, however, in formal rulemakings, determinations relating to claims for money or benefits, and applications for initial licenses if the agency has adopted procedures for submitting all evidence in written form, to the extent that the parties are not prejudiced by those procedures. Also, the agency may require a party seeking a hearing to request the hearing and to make a threshold showing that a hearing would serve its purpose. The agency may deny a hearing if no issues of material fact are in dispute.

Parties to formal adjudications are entitled under § 556(d) "to conduct such cross-examination as may be required for a full and true disclosure of the facts."

IV.   INTEGRITY OF THE DECISIONMAKING PROCESS

A.   Bias or Prejudgment of Adjudicatory Decisionmakers

A decision by a biased decisionmaker may violate due process as well as the APA.

Because some agency adjudicators, particularly agency heads, have responsibilities broader than simply adjudicating, the rules relating to disqualification of those administrative adjudicators for bias do not entirely parallel the rules relating to judges

An adjudicative decisionmaker must disqualify him- or herself, or be disqualified, from deciding any case in which the decisionmaker is biased. If a party fails to make a timely motion for disqualification, the party has waived the right to do so.

Bias or prejudgment exists when the decisionmaker has a pecuniary or other personal interest in the case, has prejudged the facts against a party, or, prior to the commencement of the hearing, had developed personal animus against a party, witness, or counsel or a group to which they belong. Bias is not established merely because the decisionmaker has rejected the claims or the testimony of a party or because the decisionmaker has fixed views about law, policy, or factual propositions not related to specific parties.

If a single member of a multimember agency was biased and was not disqualified from deciding the case, the agency's decision should be reversed, even though the biased member's vote was not necessary to the decision.

B.   Personal Responsibility of Decisionmakers

An agency decisionmaker who did not hear the presentation of evidence must become personally familiar with the issues in the case prior to rendering a decision. The decisionmaker can comply with this requirement by reading portions of the transcript and briefs, hearing oral argument, reading a report of lower-level decisionmakers, reading summaries prepared by staff members, or receiving a briefing by staff members. An agency decisionmaker may also delegate the decision to a lower-level official if such delegation is permitted by law.

Agency decisionmakers are presumed to be personally familiar with the issues of a case prior to rendering their decision. Absent evidence suggesting the decisionmaker was not familiar with the issues, it is improper to conduct discovery on the extent to which a decisionmaker familiarized him- or herself with the issues or the manner in which this occurred.

C. Prohibition on Ex Parte Communications

Interested persons outside the agency may not make, or cause to be made, an ex parte communication to an agency decisionmaker that is relevant to the merits of a formal adjudication in which they are interested. If prohibited communications occur, they must be disclosed.

"Interested person" means a person whose interest in the matter is more specific than the general interest of a member of the public.

The phrase "relevant to the merits of the proceeding" is broader than the term "fact in issue" under APA §554(d)(1). However, requests for status reports are not relevant to the merits.

The prohibition on ex parte communication covers members of the body comprising the agency (so-called agency heads), administrative law judges, or any "other employee who is or may reasonably be expected to be involved in the decisional process of the proceeding."

APA §557(d) applies only to communications from persons "outside the agency." Communications to decisionmakers from staff members inside the agency are covered by the provision on separation of functions. The president is considered to be "outside the agency" even though the agency is in the executive branch.

The APA section on ex parte communications does not constitute authority to withhold information from Congress. Nor does it extend to "disposition of ex parte matters authorized by law."

The prohibition on ex parte communication goes into effect at the earliest of the following times: (1) when the person responsible for the communication acquires knowledge that a hearing will be noticed; (2) when the proceeding is noticed for a hearing; or (3) at such time as the agency shall designate.

If an adjudicatory decisionmaker makes or receives a prohibited ex parte communication, the decisionmaker shall place in the record the prohibited ex parte communication if the communication was written, or, if it was oral, a memorandum stating the substance of the communication. In addition, the decisionmaker shall place on the record all written responses, and memoranda stating the substance of all oral responses, to such communications.

Adjudicatory decisionmakers may, consistent with the interests of justice and the policy of underlying statutes, require a party who makes or causes to be made a prohibited communication to show cause why his or her claim or interest in the proceeding should not be dismissed, denied, disregarded, or otherwise adversely affected on account of such violation. Moreover, the agency may, to the extent consistent with the interests of justice and the policy of the underlying statutes, consider a violation of the section sufficient grounds for a decision adverse to a party who knowingly violated it.

Decisions tainted by ex parte communications are voidable rather than void. A reviewing court must decide whether the agency's decisionmaking process makes the ultimate judgment of the agency unfair either to any party or to the public interest.

The APA's limitations on ex parte communications are inapplicable to informal adjudications. A court reviewing an informal adjudication should not overturn the agency action on the basis of ex parte communications unless the communications violated restrictions in a statute other than the APA or deprived a party of procedural due process under the Constitution.

D. Legislative Interference with Adjudication

Legislative pressure on adjudicators may violate the APA prohibition on ex parte contacts and may also deprive parties of their constitutional rights to due process. Claims of such violations are most likely to succeed where the congressional pressure probably influenced the decision of the adjudicators, the communication concerned disputed facts as opposed to issues of law or policy, and the particular application of pressure served no legitimate purpose, such as statutory revision or congressional oversight of administration.

E. Separation of Functions: General Rule

An agency staff member who has engaged in an adversary function in a case may not participate or advise in an adjudicatory decision in that case or a factually related adjudication. Engagement means significant and personal participation in the functions of prosecution, investigation, or advocacy.

The separation of functions requirement does not preclude agency decisionmakers from taking part in a determination to launch an investigation or issue a complaint or similar preliminary decision and later serving as a decisionmaker in the same case.

Under the APA, separation of functions does not apply in determining applications for initial licenses or to proceedings involving the validity or application of rates, facilities, or practices of public utilities or carriers.

The requirement of separation of functions does not prohibit agency heads, including members of multimember commissions, from personally engaging in an adversary function and later participating in an adjudicatory decision in the same or a factually related case. However, the individual must be an agency head at the time of both investigation and decision.

F.   Separation of Functions and Administrative Law Judges

An administrative law judge (ALJ) is not permitted to consult off the record with any person, inside or outside of the agency, concerning a fact in issue.

An ALJ may not be responsible to or subject to the supervision or direction of an agency staff member who is contemporaneously performing investigative or prosecutorial functions.

The APA's separation of functions restrictions do not apply in determining applications for initial licenses or to proceedings involving the validity or application of rates, facilities, or practices of public utilities or carriers.

G.   The Rule of Necessity

If disqualifying one or more decisionmakers would render the agency incapable of acting, those decisionmakers should not be disqualified.

V.   ADMINISTRATIVE LAW JUDGES UNDER THE ADMINISTRATIVE PROCEDURE ACT

A.   ALJ Powers and Duties

The APA confers substantial powers on ALJs in the course of presiding at hearings, including the powers to issue subpoenas and take depositions as authorized by law, to administer oaths, to receive relevant evidence, and to regulate the course of the hearing. These powers arise from the APA without the necessity of express agency delegation, and agencies are "without power to withhold [them]." They must be exercised subject to the published rules of the agency.

B.   The Selection Process

The Office of Personnel Management (OPM), the central personnel agency of the federal government, holds periodic competitions for positions as ALJs. The OPM has broad discretion in determining the method of selection; the creation and modification of these standards can be declared invalid if the OPM's actions are arbitrary and unreasonable.

C.   Inconsistent Functions

An agency cannot assign an administrative law judge to perform duties inconsistent with the duties and responsibilities of administrative law judges.

D.   Tenure

The position of administrative law judge is a tenured position, and one holding this position may be removed or disciplined only for good cause established by the Merit Systems Protection Board (MSPB) after opportunity of hearing before the Board. The MSPB itself has no authority to take action against an ALJ; it determines whether there is good cause for the particular agency to take action and, if so, what particular action the agency is allowed to take.

Actions by an ALJ that are inconsistent with the primary purpose of the APA in that they undermine confidence in the administrative adjudicatory process constitute good cause for disciplinary action. Thus, good cause for disciplinary action may include instances of bias, misconduct, incompetence, failure to perform duties, insubordination, physical incapacity, violations of statutory law or agency rules, or a refusal to follow settled precedents.

If a disciplinary action by an agency is arbitrary, politically motivated, or otherwise based on reasons that constitute an improper interference with the performance by an ALJ of his or her judicial functions, the charge cannot constitute good cause.

Disciplinary action against an ALJ may include removal or suspension.

E.   Compensation

Compensation of administrative law judges is set by the OPM at designated levels independent of agency recommendations and ratings. The OPM has the right to determine the pay level at which each ALJ is placed and the qualifications required for appointment to each level. Once an ALJ is appointed to a designated level, the method of advancement is governed by the provisions of 5 U.S.C. § 5372.

In promoting ALJs, the hiring agency decides if there is a vacancy for an ALJ and if the vacancy should be filled by promotion of a current ALJ. The OPM then decides which ALJ shall receive the promotion.

However, in cases of promoting an incumbent ALJ to Chief ALJ, the power to select is vested in the employing agency.

F.   Rotation

Administrative law judges shall be assigned to cases in rotation so far as practicable. The phrase "so far as practicable" permits a practice of categorizing cases according to level of difficulty and assigning ALJs in rotation among the categories in which they qualified. The assignment of ALJs cannot be made with the intent or effect of interfering with ALJ independence or otherwise depriving a party of a fair hearing.

G.   ALJ Performance

Under OPM regulations, an agency shall not rate the performance of an ALJ. An agency may, however, introduce managerial programs to increase the quality and production of case decisions, so long as these programs do not interfere with the decisional independence of the ALJ. Agencies may institute programs for reviewing ALJ decisions outside of the normal administrative appeal process. Agencies may also set reasonable production goals for ALJs.

H.   The Savings Clause

When a hearing is required by the APA for adjudication and the hearing is not held before the agency itself or one or more members of the body that comprises the agency, an ALJ must preside over the hearing unless the hearing is conducted "by or before boards or other employees specially provided for by or designated under statute." A statutory provision that relies on this "savings clause" to except a case from the scope of the APA must be express and clear.

VI. POST-HEARING REQUIREMENTS

A. Findings of Fact and Conclusions of Law

Agency decisions in formal adjudications shall include agency findings and conclusions, and the reasons underlying those findings and conclusions, on all material issues of fact, law, or agency discretion presented in the adjudication record. An agency need not provide a detailed and explicit weighing of each relevant consideration to accomplish these purposes. It is sufficient if the bases of its decision are reasonably discernible and a reviewing court can satisfy itself that the agency gave a "hard look" at the relevant issues. An agency's departure from its own prior decisions in a similar case or cases must be accompanied by an explanation for that departure.

B. Administrative Review

Most agencies have at least one level of internal administrative review. Such review, however, is not a constitutional right. Because constitutional due process does not require administrative review, its specification is determined by an agency's enabling act and its rules. The agency has a duty to inform disappointed parties of the means for seeking administrative review of an initial decision.

Parties seeking administrative review generally must satisfy the same conditions imposed on judicial review: they must exhaust non-appeal processes and the decision appealed must be final; they must present the administrative review authority with all of their objections to the decision below, must note all available evidence and issues in the prior proceeding, and preserve issues for review. However, in an appropriate case the administrative review authority may consider an issue sua sponte even though the issue was not raised by a party.

The adjudicatory authority of the agency resides with the agency head or heads unless it has been delegated by statute or agency regulation to another or subordinate decisionmaker. Except where an ALJ decision has become final under § 557(b) (an initial decision not timely appealed), it becomes part of the record underlying the agency's decision. Where an initial decision is appealed within an agency, the decision of the final appellate authority within the agency constitutes the agency's decision for purposes of judicial review.

An agency may adopt an initial decision by an ALJ without making independent findings or reasons.

On appeal from an initial decision, the agency has all the powers that it would have in making the initial decision, unless a statute or the agency's own rules provide otherwise. Absent such a provision, an agency owes no deference to initial decisions by an ALJ. Where the agency and ALJ disagree on the facts, the court will review the agency's, not the ALJ's, findings, unless otherwise provided by the agency's enabling statute or regulations. However, the initial decision of an ALJ is part of the record for purposes of judicial review, and a reviewing court will take it into account in judging whether the agency's decision is adequately reasoned and supported by substantial evidence.

VII. INFORMAL ADJUDICATION

A.   Basic Principles

"Informal adjudication" is the name used to denote various procedures for issuing orders when formal adjudication is not required. As discussed above in § II.A, formal adjudication is required when an agency issues an order under a statute that requires an "on-the-record" agency hearing.

B.   Informal Adjudication Procedures

Informal adjudication comprises a wide variety of agency procedures, some resembling what is traditionally thought of as adjudication and others not resembling adjudication at all. The APA contains little in the way of procedural requirements specifically targeted to informal adjudication. However, §§ 555 and 558 prescribe a number of general procedural requirements that are pertinent to informal and formal adjudication. Section 555 governs the mechanics of agency process, including the issuance of administrative subpoenas, the rights of representation to be afforded before an agency, and an agency's obligations to provide transcripts, notices of denial, and statements of reasons. Section 558 imposes certain minimal requirements on licensing proceedings and requires that all agency orders and sanctions be authorized by law. More-detailed procedures for informal adjudication are typically found in particular agency statutes and agency rules and may also be required by due process.

C.   Departures from Formal Proceedings

Informal adjudication procedures depart from the formal adjudicatory model in many respects. Subject to possible constraints imposed by due process, informal adjudication may include informal conferences, ex parte contacts, active involvement by the decisionmaker in the investigation and prosecution of the agency's case, lack of representation by counsel if there are no hearings before the agency, limited evidentiary requirements, and generally a relaxation of the formalities associated with formal adjudication. There also may be no provision for confrontation of evidence and witnesses, and there may be no discovery or transcript of the proceedings. Some informal adjudications employ procedures similar to those used in notice-and-comment rulemaking, for example by giving interested parties notice of the agency's proposed order and allowing written or oral comments without formal adjudicatory procedures.

If an agency employs notice-and-comment procedures in informal adjudication, comments may be accepted from interested persons not party to the proceedings. If the agency chooses (or is required by statute or regulation) to hold public hearings, these may actually be open meetings at which all interested persons can express their views on the matter without cross-examination or formal consideration of evidence.

D.   The *Vermont Yankee* Rule in Informal Adjudication

The *Vermont Yankee* rule prohibiting courts from imposing procedures on agencies not required by any statute or rule or the
Constitution applies to informal adjudication. Absent constitutional
concerns, federal courts may not require agencies engaged in informal
adjudication to add to the procedures required by applicable statutes
and rules such as APA §§ 555 and 558.

E.   Judicial Review of Informal Adjudication

Judicial review of final agency action in cases of informal adjudication generally is available. Unless a statute or the Constitution requires
otherwise, the standard of review of fact-findings underlying orders
issued after informal adjudication is "arbitrary, capricious, an abuse of
discretion, or otherwise not in accordance with law."

PART TWO
INFORMAL RULEMAKING

PART TWO
INFORMAL RULEMAKING

The following summarizes the procedural requirements that must precede the legally effective promulgation, amendment, or repeal of a rule by a federal agency, as imposed by the APA, other procedural statutes, and judicial decisions. Certain additional requirements imposed by executive order (primarily E.O. 12,866) are also included. Such requirements are not judicially enforceable, may be and often are waived by the relevant executive office, and are particularly subject to change. Economic impact analysis has been required for the last several presidencies in one form or another, and there is no indication that this requirement will be rescinded anytime soon.

I.   APPLICABILITY

A.   Definition of a Rule

A "rule" is an agency statement designed to implement, interpret, or prescribe law or policy or describing the organization, procedure, or practice requirements of an agency. Although the definition of rule in the APA refers to "an agency statement of general or particular applicability," "rule" is usually understood to refer to a pronouncement that is intended to address a class of situations, rather than a named individual. Certain particularized actions, such as rate-setting or the approval of a corporate reorganization, are explicitly included within the statutory definition. A rule may be prospective, retroactive, or both, but an agency normally may not issue a retroactive rule that is intended to have the force of law unless it has express authorization from Congress.

B.   Distinction between Informal and Formal Rulemaking

The procedures described here apply to "informal" (also known as "notice-and-comment") rulemaking. "Formal rulemaking" requires additional trial-type procedures, not described here but essentially the same as those described for initial licensing in the discussion of adjudication. Unless a statute expressly provides for rulemaking "on the record after opportunity for a hearing," or Congress otherwise unequivocally requires formal rulemaking, the requirements for informal rulemaking apply.

An agency engaged in informal rulemaking may provide additional procedures beyond those established by the APA, other applicable statutes, and the agency's own rules, but courts may not require it to do so.

C.   Exemptions

The following types of rules are exempt from all the procedural requirements: rules relating to public property, loans, grants, benefits, and contracts; rules relating to agency management and personnel; and rules that involve a military or foreign-affairs function of the United States. However, specific statutes may override these exemptions, and agencies may voluntarily forswear them.

The following types of rules are subject to publication and petition requirements but are exempt from the other procedural requirements set out below: rules regarding agency organization, procedure, and practice; staff manuals; interpretive rules; and general statements of policy. Courts are regularly called upon to police agency invocation of these exemptions. Especially with respect to interpretive rules and policy statements (often lumped together as "guidance"), agencies must make sure they do not treat them as binding or seek to add new requirements without seeking public comment.

An agency may also dispense with notice and comment, and/or may make a rule effective immediately, when it finds it has good cause to do so and explains its finding and reasons at the time of publication. Under time pressure, agencies, after such a finding, sometimes adopt "interim final rules" that are both immediately effective and published with an invitation to comment and propose revisions; a subsequent agency revision will treat such a rule as if it were, also, a notice of proposed rulemaking.

Failure to publish a given rule, either in the *Federal Register* or as described by 5 U.S.C. § 552(a)(2), denies to the agency any possibility of relying on it to the disadvantage of a private party, unless that party has had actual notice of the agency's position.

II. INITIATING RULEMAKING

A. Means to Initiate Rulemaking

An agency may commence a rulemaking on its own initiative, pursuant to statutory mandate, or in response to an outside petition or to suggestions from other governmental actors. Any interested person has the right to petition for the issuance, amendment, or repeal of any rule. The denial of a petition is judicially reviewable and should be at least summarily explained.

B. Developing a Proposed Rule

In developing a proposed rule, an agency may be required to evaluate and prepare appropriate written analyses of (a) overall economic costs and benefits and (b) the extent of new paperwork and information collection requirements. The agency may also be required to analyze more particularized issues, including impacts on (c) the environment; (d) small businesses; (e) state, local, and tribal governments and the private sector; (f) families; (g) private-property rights; (h) the civil justice system; (i) children's health and safety; (j) energy supply, distribution, and use; and (k) federalism. Some of the foregoing requirements are limited to economically significant rules, and some are limited to rulemaking by executive agencies. Requirements (a) through (e) are imposed by statute; requirements (f) through (k) were imposed exclusively by a series of executive orders.

Requirement (a), although now also required by the Unfunded Mandates Reform Act, was first developed by executive orders—currently, E.O. 12,866. In practice, the administration of E.O. 12,866 appears to dominate executive-branch implementation of all these requirements. Under that executive order, prior to issuing a Notice of Proposed Rulemaking, an executive agency proposing an economically significant rule must provide the Office of Information and Regulatory Affairs (OIRA), in the Office of Management and Budget (OMB), with an assessment of the proposal's costs and benefits. This analysis may, and typically does, incorporate the analyses required by other statutes and executive orders.

Before issuing a Notice of Proposed Rulemaking, an agency may issue and take comments on an Advanced Notice of Proposed Rulemaking and/or establish a negotiated rulemaking committee to negotiate and develop a proposed rule. Under the Negotiated Rulemaking Act, agencies are encouraged to explore the development of consensus proposals for rulemaking with balanced, representative committees under the guidance of a convenor specially appointed for that purpose. Such proposals, if generated, serve as proposed rules under the normal procedure.

Under the Paperwork Reduction Act, all agencies must obtain OIRA clearance of proposed informational collection requirements, including those put in place by rulemaking.

C.   Semiannual Agenda

The Regulatory Flexibility Act requires all rulemaking agencies to semiannually prepare and publish in the *Federal Register* a regulatory agenda listing all planned regulatory actions that are likely to have a significant economic impact on a substantial number of small entities. Under E.O. 12,866, all rulemaking agencies must prepare an agenda of all regulations under development or consideration. This agenda must include a Regulatory Plan identifying and justifying the most important "significant regulatory actions" the agency expects to issue in proposed or final form in the upcoming fiscal year and must be submitted to OIRA by June 1 each year. This plan is consolidated with the regulatory agenda for publication purposes.

III. NOTICE OF PROPOSED RULEMAKING AND OPPORTUNITY FOR COMMENT

A. Requirements for a Notice of Proposed Rulemaking

An agency must publish in the *Federal Register* notice of its intent to promulgate, amend, or repeal a rule. Publication in the *Federal Register* is not necessary if all persons who will be subject to the rule, if adopted, are named and have actual notice.

The Notice of Proposed Rulemaking must include (1) a statement of the time, place, and nature of any public proceedings for consideration of the proposed rule; (2) a reference to the agency's statutory authority for the rule; and (3) the proposed text of the rule, unless a description of the proposal or the subjects and issues involved will suffice to allow meaningful and informed public consideration and comment. Case law has required the agency also to make available in time for comment thereon significant data and studies it knows to be relevant to the proposed rule, including any draft analyses previously made available, as under II above.

B. Public Comment on Proposed Rule

After publication of a Notice of Proposed Rulemaking, a reasonable time must be allowed for written comments from the public. Executive orders have provided that such a comment period should normally be sixty days for significant rules. An agency may, but, unless specifically required to do so by a relevant statute, need not, provide interested persons the opportunity to present oral comments or cross-examine witnesses.

IV. THE RULEMAKING RECORD AND DECISIONMAKING PROCESS

A.   Record Requirements

The agency must maintain, and allow and facilitate public examination of, a rulemaking file (often now called a "docket") consisting of (1) all notices pertaining to the rulemaking; (2) copies or an index of written factual material, studies, and reports relied on or seriously consulted by agency personnel in formulating the proposed or final rule; (3) all written comments received by the agency; and (4) any other material specifically required by statute, executive order, or agency rule to be made public in connection with the rulemaking.

The notice-and-comment process and docketing practices have been transformed by the advent of electronic communications. The government's central rulemaking portal, www.regulations.com, allows the public to comment on any pending rulemaking, and it also serves as the home for current and past rulemaking dockets. When comments are sent directly to the agency, the agency is supposed to post them to the central portal as soon as feasible.

The obligation to disclose written factual material, studies, and reports relied on or seriously consulted by agency personnel is limited to unprivileged materials. Thus, neither a summary nor a record of predecisional internal agency policy discussions, or like contacts with government officials outside the agency or private consultants, or confidential business information, will ordinarily need to be included in the rulemaking file. Particular agency statutes or rules, however, may forbid or limit such outside communications or require that they be logged and made available to the public. The executive orders requiring economic impact analysis provoked concern about this issue, and E.O. 12,866 also includes such requirements.

B.   Decisional Process

Again, subject to the obligation to disclose factual material, studies, and reports relied on or seriously consulted, decisionmakers within an agency may freely consult with other agency personnel, government officials outside the agency, and affected persons. Particular statutes or agency regulations may impose logging requirements or other restrictions. A decisionmaker will be disqualified for prejudgment only where the person's mind is unalterably closed.

Under E.O. 12,866 (and the other impact analysis requirements imposed by statute and/or executive order), a final analysis must be prepared in advance of the final rule; that analysis is generally a part of the rulemaking record. An executive agency may not publish a significant final rule until OIRA has completed, waived, or exceeded the time limit for its review of the rule under E.O. 12,866.

A rulemaking must be completed within a reasonable time, or within the time frame, if any, set by the relevant statute. If it is not, the agency does not necessarily forfeit its ability to issue the rule, but interested persons may seek court action to compel completion of the rulemaking.

V.   THE FINAL RULE

A.   Publication of Final Rule and the Basis and Purpose of the Rule

The agency must publish the operative text of the final rule. The agency must also provide a preamble that adequately explains the justifications, purposes, and legal authority for the rule and indicates compliance with regulatory analysis requirements imposed by statute. The scope of this explanation depends on the importance and impact of the rule. The APA calls for only a "concise general statement of . . . basis and purpose." However, courts have required that, especially for rules likely to have significant economic or other impacts, the statement (a) must demonstrate that the agency seriously considered significant alternatives to its final rule, important public comments, and relevant information and scientific data, and (b) must explain the agency's rejection of any of the foregoing.

After a rule subject to OIRA review has been published, E.O. 12,866 provides that the agency and OIRA disclose specified information pertaining to the review.

If the final rule is not a "logical outgrowth" of the proposed rule, a second round of notice and comment is required.

B.   Effective Date

A substantive rule of general applicability is unenforceable unless published in the *Federal Register* and cannot ordinarily become effective less than thirty days after its publication (unless it grants an exception or relieves a restriction).

No economically significant rule can take effect (a) until sixty calendar days after the agency has submitted a copy of the rule and a concise general statement about it to both Houses of Congress and the Comptroller General and has submitted additional supporting material to the Comptroller General and made such material available to both Houses of Congress, or (b) if a joint resolution disapproving the rule is enacted. Rules relating to agency management or personnel or agency organization, procedure, or practice are exempt from this sixty-day requirement.

PART THREE
SCOPE OF REVIEW

PART THREE
SCOPE OF REVIEW

I.   GENERAL

Except where a statute § 7provides otherwise, courts generally review agency action according to the principles set forth below. These principles collectively constitute a judicial gloss on § 706 of the APA, although courts do not always describe them as such. In applying these principles, a court should distinguish among the agency's legal, factual, and policy conclusions, because different standards of review apply to each category.

If a particular challenge has not been properly preserved at the administrative level, the reviewing court has discretion not to address it. If the unpreserved challenge relates to an issue of fact or policy, the court typically is not permitted to adjudicate it (see *infra* § VI).

II.   STANDARDS OF REVIEW: STATUTORY ISSUES

A.   In General

The court will set aside an agency action if it finds that the action exceeds the authority granted, or violates limitations imposed, by a federal statute. APA § 706(2)(C).

B.   Determining Statutory Requirements—
The *Chevron* Doctrine

Where Congress has delegated to an agency the power to speak with the force of law, and the agency has, in the course of exercising that power, interpreted ambiguity in the statute that it administers, the reviewing court must afford some deference to the agency's reasonable statutory interpretation. Such deference is provided by the two-part "*Chevron* test." See *Chevron U.S.A., Inc. v. NRDC*, 467 U.S. 837 (1984).

Under step one of the *Chevron* test, the reviewing court determines whether the statutory meaning with respect to the precise issue before it is "clear" (and thus, not "ambiguous"). Step one of *Chevron* does not dictate that courts use any particular method of statutory interpretation. However, the court should use "the traditional tools of statutory construction" to determine whether the meaning of the statute is clear with respect to the precise issue before it. For most judges, these tools include examination of the text of the statute, dictionary definitions, canons of construction, statutory structure, legislative purpose, and legislative history.

If the statutory meaning on the precise issue before the court is not clear, or if the statute is silent on that issue, the court is required to defer to the agency's interpretation of the statute if that interpretation is "reasonable" or "permissible" (step two of *Chevron*).

While there is no single, established method of conducting the step two analysis, two interrelated approaches are most prominent. First, courts regularly examine the same statutory materials relied on in step one, seeking to determine whether the statute, even if subject to more than one interpretation, can support the particular interpretation adopted by the agency. For example, the court might find that the statutory context, viewed as a whole, clearly rules out the option the agency selected, or a premise on which it relied. (Some courts, however, make essentially the same inquiry within step one when they determine whether the agency interpretation violates the clear meaning of the statute. As a practical matter, the court's review of these legal issues is not affected by which step is deemed to be involved. In either case, the court is measuring the interpretation against congressionally established limitations.)

Second, in addition to engaging in conventional statutory construction, or in some cases instead of engaging in it, courts at step two of *Chevron* evaluate whether the agency, in reaching its interpretation, reasoned from statutory premises in a well-considered fashion. Courts may look, for example, to whether the interpretation is supported by a reasonable explanation and is logically coherent, or they may ask whether the agency interpretation is arbitrary or capricious in substance. In this regard, the step two inquiry tends to merge with review under the "arbitrary and capricious" standard (see *infra* § V).

C.   The Scope of *Chevron*

(1)   *Chevron* principles apply to an agency's interpretation of a statute the agency administers, where
    a.   the interpretation is embodied in a rule that has the force of law;
    b.   the interpretation was developed in the course of formal adjudication, except where the adjudicating agency's lawmaking power is limited by virtue of a "split-enforcement" statutory scheme, in which lawmaking authority over the same subject has been vested in an enforcing agency;
    c.   the interpretation was developed in the course of informal agency action if the agency's conferred authority and other statutory circumstances demonstrate that "Congress would expect the agency to be able to speak with the force of law" in taking such action, *United States v. Mead Corp.*, 533 U.S. 218, 229 (2001); or
    d.   the interstitial nature of the legal question, the related expertise of the agency, the importance of the question to administration of the statute, the complexity of that administration, and the careful consideration the agency has given the question over a long period of time indicate that *Chevron* deference is appropriate.

(2)   *Chevron* principles do not apply to agency interpretations
    a.   of statutes that apply to many agencies and are specially administered by none, such as the APA, Freedom of Information Act (FOIA), or the National Environmental Policy Act (although *Chevron* may apply to interpretations of statutes administered by two or a few agencies);

    b.   of criminal statutes where the agency's power with respect to the statute consists solely of the power to prosecute offenses in court;

    c.   that contradict the interpretation of a statute given in a controlling judicial decision if that court's opinion indicates that its interpretation follows from the unambiguous terms of the statute and thus leaves no room for agency discretion;

    d.   that represent merely the agency's litigating posture developed after the agency's decision; or

    e.   that are embodied in policy statements, manuals, enforcement guidelines, interpretive rules, and other such documents unless the agency's conferred authority and other statutory circumstances demonstrate that "Congress would expect the agency to be able to speak with the force of law" in taking such action.

(3)   Although in general courts have extended *Chevron* deference to agencies' interpretations of the boundaries of their own statutory jurisdiction, *Chevron* principles have uncertain application to an agency interpretation that significantly expands the agency's previously recognized jurisdiction.

D.   *Skidmore* Deference

Even in situations in which *Chevron* principles do not apply, such as those just mentioned, courts ordinarily will give some deference or weight to an agency's interpretation of a statute that it administers. In these circumstances, as the Supreme Court ruled in *Skidmore v. Swift & Co.*, 323 U.S. 134 (1944), the agency's view can have "power to persuade," as distinguished from "power to control." In determining whether and to what extent an agency interpretation deserves *Skidmore* deference, courts are guided by such factors as the thoroughness evident in its consideration, the validity of its reasoning, and its consistency with earlier and later pronouncements.

In various circumstances, the rigor of a court's scrutiny when it applies *Skidmore* sometimes appears to resemble *Chevron* deference, but at other times it appears significantly more intrusive. No clear pattern emerges from the cases. When faced with uncertainty as to whether its review should be governed by *Chevron* or *Skidmore*, a court will sometimes declare that it does not need to choose, because it would uphold, or would reject, the agency's interpretation under either standard.

III. STANDARDS OF REVIEW: NONSTATUTORY LEGAL ISSUES

A.   The court will set aside an agency action if it finds that the action exceeds the authority granted, or violates limitations imposed, by
1.   the Constitution;
2.   an agency rule having the force of law (as opposed to, for example, internal operating procedures);
3.   federal common law, in the rare cases in which it applies;
4.   any other source of law that is binding upon the agency, including a consent decree or other judicial order, international law, and (to the extent applicable and enforceable by their terms) executive orders.
See APA §§ 706(2)(A) (requiring invalidation of agency action "not in accordance with law"), 706(2)(B) (requiring invalidation of agency action that is "contrary to constitutional right, power, privilege, or immunity").

B.   Except as provided in subsection C, below, in resolving legal issues arising under the foregoing sources of law, courts have no established tradition of deference to any agency, although they occasionally give some weight to the agency's views.

C.   Pursuant to what is sometimes called "*Auer*" or "*Seminole Rock*" deference, a court must accept an agency's interpretation of its own regulation unless the agency's interpretation is "plainly erroneous or inconsistent with the regulation." *Auer v. Robbins*, 519 U.S. 452, 461 (1997) (quoting *Bowles v. Seminole Rock & Sand Co.*, 325 U.S. 410, 414 (1945)). The Supreme Court has applied *Auer* deference to agency interpretations, as in litigation briefs, that are not the outgrowth of any formal process within the agency as long as it appears that the interpretation reflects the agency's fair and considered judgment. A lesser degree of deference is sometimes considered appropriate where Congress has not delegated lawmaking authority to the agency or where an agency seeks deference for an interpretation of a regulation that merely parrots the language of the statute.

IV. STANDARDS OF REVIEW: ISSUES OF FACT

The following standards apply, as specified herein, when courts review agencies' findings regarding purely factual questions. These standards also are commonly used to review agency findings that may be termed "factual" but actually embody a degree of normative judgment. (Such findings present what are sometimes called questions of "ultimate fact" or of "application of law to fact," or "mixed questions of law and fact.") In reviewing these findings, a court is likely to look exclusively to the standards expounded in this section if the meaning of the law is not in dispute. Where, however, the parties do disagree about the meaning of relevant law, the reviewing court must resolve that dispute using the appropriate test for adjudicating issues of law (see *supra* §§ II, III); if the agency action survives that scrutiny, the court then applies the appropriate standard stated in this section.

A. Formal Proceedings

If the agency action resulted from a proceeding subject to 5 U.S.C. §§ 556 and 557, or otherwise is reviewed on the record of an agency hearing provided by statute, the court determines whether the agency's factual finding or premise is supported by substantial evidence in the record as a whole. APA § 706(2)(E). It is impossible to quantify "substantial evidence" precisely; one much-quoted Supreme Court formulation is "such evidence as a reasonable mind might accept as adequate to support a conclusion." This level of review is somewhat less intense than that employed when appellate courts review trial court findings of fact. In reviewing for substantial evidence, the court must consider the entire record, including the decision and factual findings of the ALJ, if any, not just those portions of the record that support the agency's findings.

B.   Trial De Novo

When the agency action resulted from a proceeding in which a statute or the Constitution requires that the facts shall be subject to trial de novo, the court makes its own, independent findings of fact and determines whether the agency action is warranted thereby. See APA § 706(2)(F). Trial de novo is available when a court reviews an agency's denial of a FOIA request, but it is otherwise rare.

C.   Other Cases

(1)   In any other case, the court determines whether the factual premise has substantial support in the administrative record viewed as a whole (although the legal standard nominally being applied is the "arbitrary and capricious" test). APA § 706(2)(A).

(2)   For these purposes, the "administrative record" consists of a file of materials that the agency maintains as the exclusive basis for its decision; or, if no such file is maintained, it consists of all unprivileged materials that were actively considered by the agency or its staff (or that were submitted by outside parties) in connection with the action under review. Where procedural law so provides, the record must also disclose oral communications between decisionmakers and outside parties.

(3)   The court may, upon a proper showing, allow discovery and other evidentiary proceedings in order to supervise the agency's compilation (but not the supplementation) of the administrative record.

D.   Findings Not Specifically Supported by the Record

Notwithstanding the requirement of record support for agency findings in formal proceedings, an agency may, with notification to the parties and opportunity to rebut, rely on officially noticed facts in a proper case. APA § 556(e). In addition, in both formal and informal proceedings, an agency need not provide more support for predictive or other judgmental facts than it can fairly be expected to have gathered at the time of the action.

V.   REVIEW OF THE EXERCISE OF AGENCY DISCRETION

The court may set aside an agency action as an abuse of discretion (alternatively known in APA parlance as the "arbitrary and capricious" test), see APA § 706(2)(A), on any of several grounds. In practice, application of these grounds varies according to the nature and magnitude of the agency action. Thus, a court will typically apply the criteria rigorously during judicial review of high-stakes rulemaking proceedings (a practice commonly termed "hard look" review), but much more leniently when reviewing a routine, uncomplicated action. A court may not impose its own policy preferences on the agency. Commonly applied bases for reversal include the following:

A.   The agency relied on factors that may not be taken into account under, or ignored factors that must be taken into account under, any authoritative source of law. (The case law often describes this ground as an element of the "arbitrary and capricious" test, although it seems more properly understood as a component of the court's legal analysis. See *supra* §§ II, III.)

B.   The action does not bear a reasonable relationship to statutory purposes or requirements.

C.   The asserted or necessary factual premises of the action do not withstand scrutiny under the relevant standard of review (see *supra* § IV).

D.   The action is unsupported by any explanation or rests upon reasoning that is seriously flawed.

E.   The agency failed, without adequate justification, to give reasonable consideration to an important aspect of the problems presented by the action, such as the effects or costs of the policy choice involved, or the factual circumstances bearing on that choice.

F.   The action, where inconsistent with prior agency policies or precedents, fails to display an awareness of the change in position, fails to explain a changed view of the facts, or fails to consider serious reliance interests that its prior policy engendered.

G.   The agency failed, without an adequate justification, to consider or adopt an important alternative solution to the problem addressed in the action.

H.   The agency failed to consider substantial arguments, or respond to relevant and significant comments, made by the participants in the proceeding that gave rise to the agency action.

I.   The agency has imposed a sanction that is greatly out of proportion to the magnitude of the violation.

J.   The action fails in other respects to rest upon reasoned decisionmaking.

VI.   ANCILLARY ISSUES CONCERNING AGENCY EXPLANATIONS

In order to decide whether an agency action violates applicable standards of review, as set forth above, courts examine material portions of the agency's own proffered rationale. They normally will allow an agency to defend its action only on the basis of reasons articulated prior to judicial review and will not supply their own rationale for discretionary agency conduct or speculate as to the conceivable purposes underlying the action. A court may deem an error in reasoning to be harmless error if the agency clearly would have reached the same result even if it had not made the error.

The court ascertains the agency's rationale as follows:

(1)   An explanation issued contemporaneously with an agency action is treated as containing the agency's actual rationale for taking the action, unless the party challenging the action impeaches

the explanation with a strong showing of bad faith or improper behavior.

(2) Where an agency action is not accompanied by a contemporaneous explanation, the court may investigate the agency's rationale by receiving evidence, though this is rare. Under these circumstances there is no presumption as to whether the post hoc explanation tendered by the agency to the court expresses the agency's original rationale. In attempting to identify the agency's actual, though not contemporaneously articulated, rationale, courts generally avoid direct scrutiny of the agency's decision-making process and rely on the representations of counsel, affidavits from relevant officials, and extrinsic evidence rather than depositions, interrogatories, and courtroom testimony.

VII. PROCEDURAL ISSUES

The foregoing standards also apply to allegations that an agency violated procedural law in taking the action under review, see APA § 706(2)(D), with the applicable standard of review depending on whether the allegation rests on the agency's organic statute, the APA, agency regulations, etc. The court presumes the procedural regularity of agency action, but a person may come forward with facts to prove the contrary. An action will not be set aside because of a procedural error that plainly did not influence the outcome of the agency proceeding. APA § 706 (final sentence).

VIII. AGENCY DELAY

A court will compel agency action unlawfully withheld or unreasonably delayed, APA § 706(1), though such a claim can proceed only where a plaintiff asserts that an agency failed to take a discrete action that it is *required* to take. An agency's delay in completing a pending action for which there is no statutory deadline may not be held unlawful unless the delay is unreasonable in light of such considerations as the agency's need to set priorities among lawful objectives, the challenger's interest in prompt action, and any relevant indications of legislative intent. In considering such challenges, courts are deferential to agencies' allocations of their own limited resources.

IX. REMEDY

As noted in the foregoing sections, in general a reviewing court will set aside agency action that does not meet the standards described, instead of mandating a specific disposition of its own design. When an agency's exercise of discretion cannot be upheld on the basis of the agency's rationale, or no rationale can be discerned, or if the agency so requests, the court will almost always remand the action so that the agency can provide further justification. When remanding, a court normally will vacate the agency's action, except in special circumstances. Such circumstances may exist where (1) the court discerns a substantial probability that the agency can cure its error on remand and (2) the challenging party's interest in obtaining relief from the agency's decision is clearly outweighed by the substantial adverse impact that vacation would have on private persons who have reasonably relied on the agency action being remanded.

THE AVAILABILITY OF JUDICIAL REVIEW OF ADMINISTRATIVE ACTION

PART FOUR
THE AVAILABILITY OF JUDICIAL REVIEW
OF ADMINISTRATIVE ACTION

I. OVERVIEW OF PREREQUISITES TO JUDICIAL REVIEW

A. Statutory Basis for Subject Matter Jurisdiction and Venue

The APA itself does not provide jurisdiction in suits seeking review of federal administrative action, but the federal-question statute, 28 U.S.C. § 1331, generally does. General federal-question jurisdiction in district court does not apply, however, where special jurisdictional statutes such as the Hobbs Act, 28 U.S.C. § 2342, provide exclusive jurisdiction for review of specified classes of cases in the courts of appeals.

Under the generally applicable venue statute, 28 U.S.C. § 1391(e), venue is proper for a suit against an officer, an agency, or the United States "in any judicial district in which: (1) a defendant in the action resides, or (2) the cause of action arose, or (3) any real property involved in the action is situated, or (4) the plaintiff resides if no real property is involved in the action." This is a default provision that may be superseded by venue provisions in a special jurisdictional statute.

B. Waiver of Sovereign Immunity

Section 702 of the APA waives sovereign immunity of the federal government for judicial review of agency action where the plaintiff is seeking relief other than money damages. This waiver applies regardless of whether a petitioner invokes the APA's cause of action or some other cause of action. It also permits a suit seeking a financial award that does not technically constitute "money damages."

A claimant seeking money damages from the federal government must invoke a waiver of sovereign immunity other than § 702. Examples of such waivers include (a) provisions in agency enabling acts that authorize an agency to "sue and be sued"; (b) the Federal Tort Claims Act (FTCA), 28 U.S.C. §§ 1346(b), 2671–80, which waives sovereign immunity for certain tort claims; and (c) the Tucker Act, 28 U.S.C. § 1491, which applies, most importantly, to contract and takings claims.

C.   Official Immunity

A suit against an agency official in her official capacity is functionally identical to a suit against the government and is subject to the same principles of sovereign immunity.

A suit against an agency official in her personal capacity implicates a different set of immunity doctrines. As injunctive relief is generally available directly against the government under § 702 of the APA, the primary significance of personal-capacity suits is that they create a potential path for plaintiffs to seek money damages.

The Federal Employees Liability Reform and Tort Compensation Act of 1988 (the "Westfall Act") provides that federal officials are immune from common-law tort liability for actions taken within the scope of their employment. 28 U.S.C. § 2679(b)(1). Where the attorney general certifies that the defendant was acting within the scope of her employment, the United States is substituted as defendant. 28 U.S.C. § 2679(d)(1). Whether the United States has waived sovereign immunity is then determined according to the terms of the FTCA.

The Westfall Act does not immunize officials from constitutional torts or from claims that they have violated federal statutes that authorize a cause of action. Executive officials, however, are generally protected from suits for civil damages for such claims by the doctrine of "qualified immunity." This doctrine blocks claims for damages arising from an official's performance of discretionary functions so long as the official's conduct did not violate clearly established statutory or constitutional rights. A right is clearly established for the purpose of this test if a reasonable officer should have understood that her conduct was illegal given the particular facts she confronted. Courts have accorded absolute immunity to certain officials in light of their special functions. For instance, administrative law judges enjoy absolute immunity from damages liability allegedly arising from their judicial acts.

D.   Cause of Action or Defense

Many specific statutes authorize judicial review of particular types of federal agency action. An agency's enabling act may, for instance, contain a set of provisions establishing parameters for review of rules issued pursuant to that act's authority. Review pursuant to such provisions is sometimes characterized as a "special statutory proceeding." Often, the jurisdictional provisions for a special statutory review proceeding assign subject matter jurisdiction to courts of appeals (especially the D.C. Circuit).

In the absence of a special statutory review scheme, parties may seek review under APA §§ 702–704, which provide a general cause of action for parties "adversely affected or aggrieved by agency action" for which "there is no other adequate remedy in court."

Where neither a specific statute nor the APA provides a cause of action, parties may obtain review by seeking various forms of relief, including equitable relief under a federal court's general equity jurisdiction, 28 U.S.C. § 1331, declaratory relief under the Declaratory Judgment Act, 28 U.S.C. § 2201, and mandamus under 28 U.S.C. § 1361. (These forms of review, as well as review sought under the APA without authorization by a more specific statute, are sometimes described as instances of "nonstatutory review." This usage is misleading, however, because almost all of these forms of review rest on a statutory foundation.)

In rare circumstances, a plaintiff may sue an agency official in her *personal* capacity for a constitutional tort in a *"Bivens* action." See *Bivens v. Six Unknown Named Agents of Federal Bureau of Narcotics*, 403 U.S. 388 (1971). The Supreme Court has narrowly defined the availability of the

Bivens cause of action, and it is not available where Congress has provided an adequate statutory alternative.

Rather than challenge an agency action affirmatively, under many circumstances a party may instead raise the invalidity of an agency action as a defense in a subsequent enforcement proceeding based on that agency action. The existence of a prior, adequate, and exclusive opportunity for judicial review may, however, cut off this right to raise the invalidity of the agency action as a defense in an enforcement proceeding. Cf. § II.D, Statutory Deadlines.

E.   Reviewability

Doctrines of reviewability block judicial review of certain types of claims that would otherwise appear to fall within the scope of the APA's general cause of action. More particularly: (a) the APA's cause of action applies only to challenges to "agency action"—and not everything an agency does satisfies the APA's technical meaning of this phrase; (b) Congress may by statute preclude review of certain types of agency action; and (c) courts regard some agency actions as unreviewable because they are "committed to agency discretion by law." See § III, Reviewability.

F.   Timing Doctrines

A complex set of timing doctrines limits access to the courts for judicial review of agency action. These include the following:

Finality: In general, courts will review only final agency actions. Agency action is final if it (1) is consummated and (2) determines rights or obligations or otherwise carries legal consequences.

Exhaustion: Parties generally must pursue available intra-agency remedies, such as an appeal to higher agency authorities, before seeking judicial review.

Ripeness: Courts will normally not review a matter that is not "ripe," meaning that the issues raised in the case must be "fit" for review, and delaying review must cause hardship to the plaintiff.

Statutory deadlines: Many agency enabling acts limit the time period for petitioning for review of agency actions. However, courts generally construe such statutes to mean that even after the deadline has passed, the defendant in an enforcement proceeding may challenge a rule on the grounds that it is unconstitutional or exceeds the agency's statutory authority.

Primary jurisdiction: Courts sometimes invoke this doctrine to stay proceedings that fall within their original jurisdiction, so as to permit an agency to examine an issue that falls within its special competence but that it has not yet addressed.

For further discussion of these timing doctrines, see § II.

G. Standing—Constitutional, Prudential, and Statutory

The term "standing" covers three quite different concepts. First, for a challenge to administrative action to proceed in federal court, at least one plaintiff must demonstrate *constitutional standing*. To do so, a plaintiff must show that she has suffered an "injury in fact"—a legally cognizable injury. She must also show that this injury is fairly traceable to the defendant's conduct and that a favorable court order would likely redress it. Second, in certain circumstances, judge-made *prudential standing* doctrines deny standing to a plaintiff who satisfies constitutional standing requirements, as, for example, when the plaintiff sues to protect the rights of a third party rather than her own. Third, the doctrine of *statutory standing* inquires whether a statute authorizes a particular type of plaintiff to seek judicial review of agency action. Most important, a litigant may invoke the APA's cause of action under § 702 only if she is "adversely affected or aggrieved by agency action within the meaning of the relevant statute."

For further discussion of these standing doctrines, see § IV.

II.   TIMING OF JUDICIAL REVIEW

A. Finality

Administrative law presumes that judicial review should await final agency action; interlocutory review is generally unavailable. The APA codifies this presumption at § 704, which provides, "[a]gency action made reviewable by statute and final agency action for which there is no adequate remedy in a court are subject to judicial review."

Agency action is "final" for APA purposes if two conditions are met. First, the action must not be tentative or interlocutory, but rather the "consummation" of the agency's decisionmaking. Issuance of an administrative complaint, for example, does not satisfy this first condition.

Second, the action must determine rights or obligations, or create legal consequences. This condition implicates the following problem: certain types of agency rules—interpretive rules and policy statements—do not carry the force of law. It might seem that such rules cannot constitute "final agency action" because they do not carry legal consequences. In practice, however, interpretive rules and policy statements often have significant impact on both regulated parties and the beneficiaries of regulation. This fact suggests that the finality requirement should not immunize these types of agency action from judicial review. Thus, agency actions have sometimes been deemed "final" for judicial review purposes where the decision appears binding as a practical matter—even if the agency has characterized the decision as nonbinding (e.g., by labeling it as "informal guidance").

Where an agency action is not final and no specific statute authorizes interlocutory review, a party may obtain review of the action in two ways. First, the party may be able to seek so-called nonstatutory review outside of the APA, but only if the agency action is clearly in excess of the agency's delegated powers or the ongoing action plainly cannot result in a valid agency order. Otherwise, the party may obtain review of all preliminary, procedural, or intermediate agency action or rulings on review of the final agency action.

B.   Exhaustion of Administrative Remedies

An agency action may be considered "final" even though opportunities remain for seeking further review of the action within the agency itself. Nonetheless, where the *exhaustion* doctrine applies, it requires a plaintiff to seek relief from all available and adequate administrative remedies, including intra-agency appellate remedies, prior to seeking judicial review.

In some contexts, Congress specifies exhaustion requirements by statute. Where Congress has not done so, courts determine whether to require exhaustion by balancing the needs of the reviewing court for judicial economy and an adequate record, the needs of the agency for autonomy and for a fair opportunity to apply its expertise, and the hardship to the plaintiff of denying review. The ordinary litigation cost of exhausting the administrative remedy is not sufficient hardship to render that remedy inadequate.

The Supreme Court has identified several sets of circumstances in which a plaintiff's interest in prompt judicial review strongly favors excusing exhaustion. These include (1) where requiring exhaustion would cause undue prejudice, perhaps due to unreasonable deadlines for administrative review; (2) where the agency lacks authority to grant effective relief; and (3) where the administrative body is biased or has predetermined the issue.

Section 704 of the APA carves out an exception to the courts' "common-law" authority to impose an exhaustion requirement on plaintiffs invoking the APA's cause of action. Unless expressly required by statute, a party seeking review pursuant to the APA of otherwise final agency action need not pursue any process for agency reconsideration of its decision. However, an agency may require exhaustion of any intra-agency appeals, provided (1) it imposes this requirement by rule and (2) it provides that the agency action is inoperative during the time of the appeal. In practice, most agencies do make use of this option when it is available.

In both APA and non-APA cases, the courts have frequently refused to consider issues that were not first raised before the agency. Courts

enforce such *issue exhaustion* more stringently where the parties are
expected to develop the issues in an adversarial proceeding than in
circumstances in which they review the results of nonadversarial, informal hearings.

Some courts have also applied the issue-exhaustion doctrine to the
notice-and-comment rulemaking process. Under this approach, a party
that fails to raise an objection to a rule during notice and comment
may not press that objection on direct judicial review of the rule unless
(1) another party made the objection or (2) the agency's decision indicates that it did in fact consider the issue.

Even where courts do not apply the issue-exhaustion doctrine,
because the review of agency action under the "arbitrary and capricious" standard of § 706(2)(A) is limited to the record before the agency
at the time of its decision, the agency's action may well be deemed reasonable in the absence of an argument that was not presented to the
agency. Thus, the absence of an argument at the administrative level
may affect the substance, if not the availability, of review.

C. Ripeness

To determine whether agency action is ripe for judicial review,
courts balance (1) "the fitness of the issues for judicial decision" and (2)
"the hardship to the parties of withholding court consideration." The
Supreme Court has also advised courts to consider whether judicial
intervention would unduly interfere with subsequent agency action.

The *fitness* inquiry largely turns on whether delaying judicial
review until a rule has been applied to a particular, concrete situation
could develop a factual record that would aid judicial resolution of the
legality of the rule. Purely legal issues are thus typically, though not
always, "fit" for review.

The *hardship* inquiry largely turns on whether a rule requires
an immediate and costly change to a regulated party's "primary
conduct"—i.e., its day-to-day business. Thus, a rule requiring pharma-
ceutical firms to change their labeling practices or face possible civil
and criminal penalties satisfied the hardship prong of ripeness. By

contrast, a rule specifying that manufacturers of color additives must permit regulators to inspect their facilities on request did not.

Mere uncertainty on the challenger's part about the legality of a rule does not constitute hardship for the purpose of ripeness analysis.

Agency statements concerning how to implement or interpret a statute that the agency does not administer are unlikely to constitute hardship for the purpose of demonstrating ripeness.

D.   Statutory Deadlines for Review of Rules

Many enabling acts provide for short time limits (e.g., sixty days) for review of agency action—especially rules. In the absence of such a time limit, a six-year statute of limitations generally applies to challenges to agency action. Courts nonetheless allow post-deadline judicial review of agency rules under some circumstances. The availability of judicial review depends on whether the challenge is substantive or procedural as well as on whether the statutory time limit at issue expressly precludes untimely review.

Even after a statutory deadline has run, courts permit parties defending against application of a rule in an enforcement proceeding to challenge the rule on the substantive grounds that it is unconstitutional or exceeds the agency's statutory authority.

At least in those cases where a statutory time limit does not expressly preclude later judicial review, a party may also pursue these types of substantive challenges after a statutory deadline by making them the basis for a petition to revise or revoke the rule. If the agency denies this rulemaking petition, the party may then seek review of this denial. Such review is limited to issues considered in the denial decision and thus usually does not encompass factual or discretionary determinations underlying the original rule.

By contrast, courts generally bar post-deadline procedural challenges to rules, regardless of whether they are raised first as a defense in an enforcement proceeding or via a petition for a new rulemaking.

Courts have held that a statutory deadline for review does not begin to run until a rule is ripe for review. A party wishing to challenge a rule should at least try to do so within the statutory time period, because courts have also held that mere speculation that a challenge is unripe does not excuse an untimely petition.

An agency may restart an expired statutory time limit on judicial review by "reopening" its consideration of an earlier action by either explicitly or implicitly undertaking to reexamine it.

E.   Primary Jurisdiction

Primary jurisdiction applies when claims properly cognizable in court contain one or more issues within the special competence of an administrative agency. In such cases, the court enables a referral to the agency, staying further proceedings so as to give the parties reasonable opportunity to seek an administrative ruling. In cases of mandatory primary jurisdiction, an agency ruling is required, and the court cannot proceed with the case until the agency has acted. In cases where an agency ruling is not required but the court might benefit from the expertise of the agency, the court may make a referral but also provide that if the agency has not ruled after a certain time the court will proceed without the agency ruling.

In determining whether to invoke the doctrine of primary jurisdiction, courts consider (1) whether the issues in a case implicate an agency's expertise or discretion, (2) whether the issues need a uniform resolution that the agency is best situated to provide, and (3) whether the referral to the administrative agency will impose undue delays or costs on the litigants.

III. REVIEWABILITY

A.   "Agency Action" as a Limit on Review

The APA's cause of action applies only to "agency action." Section 551(13) defines "agency action" as including "the whole or a part of an agency rule, order, license, sanction, relief, or the equivalent or denial thereof, or failure to act." Given this expansive list, the APA's definition of "agency action" rarely blocks judicial review of an agency's affirmative action or its denial of a request for action (e.g., review of a rule or a denial of a petition for rulemaking).

The APA cause of action cannot be invoked to make a broad, programmatic attack on an agency's general work as opposed to an attack on a specific "agency action." For instance, an environmental group could not invoke the APA to challenge a Bureau of Land Management "program" in the absence of a specific agency action pursuant to that program.

The APA's inclusion of "failure to act" in the definition of "agency action" presents an interpretive challenge. At any given time, any given agency is failing to take an infinite number of actions—not all of which should count as "agency actions" subject to judicial review under the APA. The Supreme Court has solved this puzzle by holding that "failure to act" as used by § 551(13) includes only failures to take the "discrete" types of agency actions listed earlier in that subsection (e.g., failure to adopt a rule or to issue an order).

B.   Statutory Preclusion or Limitation of Review

Section 701(a)(1) of the APA recognizes that Congress may by statute preclude judicial review. The Supreme Court has never decided whether the Constitution limits this preclusive power. In part to avoid that question, courts will often work hard to interpret statutory language to avoid preclusive effect, requiring "clear and convincing evidence of a contrary legislative intent" to overcome the general presumption of judicial review.

Statutory preclusion of judicial review need not be expressed so long as the requisite congressional intent to preclude is "fairly discernible" from a statutory scheme. The Court has found implicit preclusion where judicial review on behalf of a particular group would "severely disrupt" a complex and delicate administrative scheme.

Courts are especially reluctant to find statutory preclusion where review implicates constitutional questions or the legality of a rule. By contrast, courts are quicker to find preclusion where only issues of fact or of application of law to fact are at issue.

Where Congress restricts judicial review to particular courts or times by adopting special statutory review procedures, courts generally presume that Congress intends these procedures to be the exclusive means for review.

C. Matters Committed to Agency Discretion

Section 701(a)(2) of the APA recognizes that the APA's cause of action is not available "to the extent that . . . agency action is committed to agency discretion by law." This exception to the APA's general presumption of review is narrow. The Supreme Court has stated that this exception applies where statutes are written in such broad terms that there is, in effect, "no law to apply." More broadly, the Court has recognized that there are certain categories of administrative decision that are unreviewable as a matter of tradition. Functional inquiries regarding the desirability of judicial review also come into play—though not always expressly.

For example, agency decisions regarding how to allocate lump-sum appropriations are committed to agency discretion by law. In reaching this conclusion, the Supreme Court cited tradition and also noted that such allocations require complicated balancing of many factors and determining agency priorities—tasks best handled by agencies, not courts.

Likewise, agency decisions declining to initiate enforcement actions are presumptively committed to agency discretion by law. This presumption is based on judicial respect for prosecutorial discretion and for an agency's discretion in allocating its resources. Congress can, however, overcome this presumption by providing sufficient standards limiting agency enforcement discretion to guide review in a particular case. Also, where an agency refusal to initiate an enforcement action is based on statutory interpretation, the agency's inaction can usually be reviewed, at least if it is expressed in a written policy. (Notably, the presumption against review of nonenforcement does not apply to denial of a petition for rulemaking.)

Section 701(a)(2)'s exemption to review applies only "to the extent" that agency action is committed to agency discretion. As a result, some issues raised by an action may be reviewable while others are not. The Supreme Court has, for instance, held that a constitutional claim raised in connection with termination of a government employee was reviewable but that a statutory claim was not. Similarly, even where the substance of an agency's decision is committed to agency discretion, the procedure applicable to the action may not be.

IV. STANDING

A. Overview

The doctrine of "standing" determines whether a particular litigant is entitled to an adjudication of the particular claims asserted. These requirements are imposed by the Constitution, the courts as a matter of judicial discretion, and Congress.

B. Constitutional Requirements

Article III's limitation of the judicial power to "cases" and "controversies" implies three standing requirements. First, the plaintiff must have suffered an "injury in fact"—an invasion of a legally protected interest that is (a) concrete and particularized and (b) actual or imminent, not conjectural or hypothetical. Second, there must be a causal connection between the conduct complained of and the injury—the injury has to be fairly traceable to the challenged action of the defendant, and not the result of the independent action of some third party not before the court. Third, it must be likely that the injury will be redressed by a favorable decision.

1.   *Injury*

a.   *The Constitutional Injury-in-Fact Requirement: In General*

The basic Article III requirement is "injury in fact." Constitutionally cognizable injuries include not only harms to person or property
and economic harm but also harm to nonmonetary intangible interests. For example, so long as it is individually experienced, harm to
environmental, recreational, or aesthetic interests can support standing.
The injury must be actual or imminent, not conjectural or hypothetical.
Mere ideological objection to government action does not constitute a
constitutionally cognizable injury.

In addition to the kinds of harm that would have been recognized
at common law, violations of some rights created by statute can also
qualify as injury for purposes of standing. For example, violation of a
statutory right to obtain certain information can constitute injury. However, not all rights created by statute can so qualify. For example, denial
of a statutory right to comment on a proposed rule is not injury sufficient for standing.

The right of a prevailing party to claim a statutory bounty satisfies
the injury-in-fact requirement; entitlement to attorney's fees or litigation costs does not.

The Supreme Court has suggested that when states are plaintiffs
suing on their own behalf, as opposed to *parens patriae*, special concerns
are involved that may lessen traditional standing requirements.

b.   *Injury from Violation of Procedural Requirements*

When a challenged agency action harms an underlying substantive interest of the plaintiff, the plaintiff has standing to challenge the
agency's failure to follow legally required procedures even though she
cannot prove that the procedural error actually changed the substantive outcome. For example, a taxpayer whose tax liability is increased
by a new regulation can challenge the adequacy of the notice of proposed rulemaking, even though it cannot be shown that adequate
notice would have resulted in a more favorable regulation. However, she may be required to show that a more favorable regulation is

possible. Cognizable injury cannot arise from a procedural violation without a showing that the action taken harms or endangers a concrete substantive interest of the plaintiff.

Apparently, the statutory right to attend meetings and otherwise have access to government proceedings, such as under the Government in the Sunshine Act and the Federal Advisory Committee Act, are sufficiently similar to substantive rights to be treated as such. FOIA rights and voter rights to certain information under the Federal Election Campaign Act are also substantive rights, denial of which will support standing without regard to proof of harm to a particular, underlying substantive interest.

c.   *Generalized Grievances vs. Harm to Informational Rights and Other Broadly Shared Interests*

A "generalized grievance" is not injury sufficient to confer standing. Thus, harm to the general interest shared by all citizens in the government conforming its conduct to law is not a judicially cognizable injury. Accordingly, a statute purporting to allow "any person" to challenge agency action cannot authorize suit by a plaintiff without some distinct, constitutionally cognizable injury. However, a person who suffers a concrete, particularized harm does satisfy the injury requirement even though many other persons do or could suffer the same harm. Statutes can create and/or protect broadly shared interests, harm to which can constitutionally support standing. For example, individual voters can vindicate a concrete, though widely shared, right to election-finance information required by statute to be made public. Similarly, an individual denied access to government information or to an agency meeting has standing to challenge the denial, even though all citizens have an identical right of access. The widely shared injury, while satisfying constitutional standing requirements, may raise prudential standing concerns.

d.   *Risk as Injury*

The extent to which risk of harm can constitute injury for standing purposes is not clear. On the one hand, the Supreme Court has denied standing to an organization to sue on behalf of its members when it did not show that a *specific* member was threatened with an imminent concrete harm, even though it was virtually certain that *some* member would suffer a concrete harm in the foreseeable future. On the other hand, the Court found standing on behalf of organic alfalfa farmers to challenge the deregulation of genetically modified alfalfa because of the significant risk that the lack of regulation would lead to contamination of the farmers' crops. The fact that the farmers had already undertaken activities and expended funds to avoid the risk was apparently important to the Court's conclusion. In yet a third case, the Court dismissed a claim by persons challenging the constitutionality of a statute authorizing certain government electronic surveillance because it was not "certainly impending" that they would be subject to it, even though there was clearly a significant risk that they would be. The lower courts' decisions regarding risk as injury are in tension, with the D.C. Circuit holding that for increased risk to support standing there must be both (i) a substantial increase in the risk of harm and (ii) a substantial probability of actual harm with that increase taken into account. Other circuits have generally been more receptive to considering any significant increase in risk of physical harm as sufficient cognizable injury.

e.   *Taxpayer Standing*

In general, a taxpayer does not suffer cognizable injury because the federal government spends money in a manner objectionable to the taxpayer. The one limited exception involves federal appropriations for religious purposes. Although the doctrinal basis for this exception has been undermined over the years, the foundational decision has continually been distinguished rather than overruled.

2.   *Causation and Redressability*

The constitutional requirements of *causation* and *redressability*—often together referred to as "nexus"—ensure that there is at least a reasonable probability that the plaintiff's injury was caused by the defendant and will be remedied by the relief requested from the court.

Although stated as distinct requirements, causation and redressability are typically analyzed in tandem because it is rare that one exists without the other. However, if the court's remedial options are limited by statute or other law, the injury may indeed be traceable to the defendant's action, but not redressable by the available remedies. For example, a plaintiff who has suffered an environmental injury caused by the defendant will be denied standing on redressability grounds where the wrongdoing had ceased before the suit was filed, the plaintiff cannot demonstrate a reasonable likelihood that it will recur, and the only statutory remedies are prospective injunctive relief and civil penalties payable to the government.

Analysis of causation and redressability tends to be very fact specific, and in general there is no ready formula for predicting when a court will conclude that the causal chain has become too uncertain or attenuated. Cases attempting to challenge either favorable tax treatment of a third party or decisions not to prosecute appear to follow a pattern of dismissal on the basis of an absence of either causation or redressability.

Whether causation and redressability exist can be highly dependent upon how the injury is defined. For example, if the harm to a plaintiff challenging an affirmative-action program is defined as not obtaining the relevant position or contract, the plaintiff will rarely have standing, since almost never would a particular disappointed applicant be able to show it would have obtained the benefit but for the challenged program. However, the Court instead defines the injury in such cases as a lack of opportunity to compete for the desired outcome according to permissible criteria, a definition that eliminates problems of causation or redressability.

A similar definitional issue is posed by the suggestion, advanced by some judges, that complaints by regulatory beneficiaries categorically present difficult causation and redressability problems not faced by regulated entities. For example, it has been argued that consumers who can satisfy the particularized injury requirement and wish to challenge

an agency's failure to adopt more rigorous fuel economy standards
for automobiles must also show that if a more demanding rule were
adopted, manufacturers would change their designs rather than pay
noncompliance penalties. Because the standard for redressability is
only that the favorable court decision would "likely" redress (or avoid)
the injury, the plaintiff should have to show only that it is likely that
the manufacturer will comply with the law.

Complaints about procedural violations provide another example.
If the injury is defined as the actual agency decision, the plaintiff will
normally not satisfy standard nexus requirements, since it will be possible, even likely, that the agency could have reached, and on remand
will reach, the same outcome even following proper procedures. The
Court, however, has made clear that when the alleged violation is procedural, the normal standards for redressability do not apply. It suffices
if the procedures exist to protect a concrete interest of the plaintiff and
a favorable outcome on the merits will be possible if the correct procedures are followed.

Redressability issues can also arise under citizen suit provisions
that provide only injunctive relief and payment of civil penalties to the
government when the complained-of action has ceased after filing of
the action, making an injunction inappropriate. While arguably, pay-
ing civil penalties to the government does not redress the injury to the
citizen plaintiff, the Court has said that such penalties deter future violations and therefore satisfy the redressability requirement.

C. Associational Standing

An association has standing in its own right if it satisfies the above
constitutional tests. In addition, an association has standing to sue
on behalf of its members when (a) one or more identified members
would have standing to sue in their own right; (b) the interests it seeks
to protect are germane to the organization's purpose; and (c) neither
the claim asserted nor the relief requested requires the participation
of individual members in the lawsuit. The second of these criteria is
construed very leniently. The third effectively limits associations suing

on behalf of their members to declaratory or injunctive relief, because if the redress required the payment of monetary damages, the persons to whom the damages would be paid would have to be parties themselves.

D. Prudential Standing Requirements

Three judicially self-imposed "prudential" restrictions further limit standing beyond the constitutional minima. Congress may, by statute, override prudential restrictions on standing.

First, parties cannot raise claims or defenses that rest on a third party's legal rights (the *jus tertii* limitation). The *jus tertii* prohibition plays an important role in constitutional litigation but has not been very significant in limiting judicial review of agency action under the APA or specific organic statutes. A litigant attempting to challenge government action on grounds that it violates the constitutional rights of a third party may be prohibited from doing so unless (1) the third party has suffered an injury in fact; (2) the litigant and the third party stand in some close relationship; and (3) "some hindrance" impedes the third party's ability to assert her own rights.

Second the plaintiff's interests must be within the "zone of interests" regulated or protected by the constitutional or statutory provision relied upon. In challenges to agency action, this requirement is subsumed under the APA requirements discussed in § IV.E.

Finally, the Court has sometimes stated that "generalized grievances" are precluded by prudential standing requirements. However, other cases have distinguished between "generalized grievances," which are not injuries for Article III purposes, and "widely shared" injuries, which satisfy Article III's standing requirement, but which perhaps should be left to the political process to rectify. Whenever Congress has created a cause of action that allowed persons suffering generalized grievances to sue, the Court has always held that the limitation was constitutional rather than prudential.

E.   Statutory Standing

The general statutory standing requirement for review of agency action under the APA is codified in § 702, which provides that "[a] person suffering legal wrong because of agency action, or adversely affected or aggrieved by agency action within the meaning of a relevant statute, is entitled to judicial review thereof." Although this language significantly broadened pre-APA availability of review to challenge agency action, it does not confer standing to the limits of what is constitutionally possible. In addition to showing that she has suffered a constitutionally cognizable injury caused by the agency's action, the plaintiff relying upon § 702 must show that her injury is "arguably within the zone of interests to be protected or regulated by the statute . . . in question." This concept is more fully discussed in § I.B, *supra.*

Individual regulatory statutes may contain their own statutory standing provisions. Statutory language authorizing challenge by "any person aggrieved" has traditionally been interpreted to confer standing to the full extent of Article III, without regard to such prudential limitations as the zone-of-interests requirement. Citizen-suit provisions (e.g., those conferring standing on "any person" without further requirements) are usually given the same interpretation. Other kinds of statutory standing provisions are typically construed to incorporate the zone-of-interests test and other prudential requirements absent evidence of a different legislative intent.

FREEDOM OF INFORMATION, SUNSHINE, ADVISORY COMMITTEES

PART FIVE
FREEDOM OF INFORMATION, SUNSHINE, ADVISORY COMMITTEES

I. THE FREEDOM OF INFORMATION ACT

A. Overview

The Freedom of Information Act (FOIA), 5 U.S.C. § 552, establishes a presumption that all records of governmental agencies are accessible to the public unless they are specifically exempted from disclosure by FOIA or another statute.

FOIA imposes the following tripartite scheme of disclosure.

1. *Federal Register Publication Requirements*

Section 552(a)(1) requires agencies to publish in the *Federal Register* descriptions of agency organization, procedures for the public to obtain information, statements of agency function, rules of procedure, descriptions of agency forms, substantive rules of general applicability and statements of general policy, and any changes in material required to be published. Where a matter is required to be published in the *Federal Register* and is not so published, no person may in any manner be required to resort to, or be adversely affected by, the matter except to the extent that the person had actual and timely notice of the matter. However, matter reasonably available to the class of persons affected thereby is deemed published in the *Federal Register* when incorporated by reference therein with the approval of the director of the *Federal Register*.

2. *Public Availability Requirements*

Section 552(a)(2) requires that agencies make available for public inspection or copying (or for sale) certain basic agency records that, while not subject to the publication requirement of § 552(a)(1), are to be made available in agency reading rooms and (for records created on or after November 1, 1996) in "electronic" reading rooms accessible by computer. Four categories of records are subject to this disclosure requirement: (a) final opinions in agency adjudications; (b) statements of policy and interpretations not published in the *Federal Register*; (c) administrative and staff manuals that affect the public; and (d) records processed and disclosed under a FOIA request that "the agency determines have become or are likely to become the subject of subsequent requests for substantially the same records." Material required to be made publicly available may be used by the agency only if indexed or made available or published, or if the party affected otherwise has timely notice of the materials.

3. *Records Disclosed on Request*

All other records unless exempt from required disclosure under § 552(b) or excluded from FOIA coverage under § 552(c) must be disclosed upon request. Disclosure is to be effected pursuant to published agency rules. The bulk of FOIA litigation, and of the remainder of § I, involves this provision.

B. Mechanics of Operation

FOIA provides that any person, including corporations; associations; and foreign persons, entities, and governments, may request agency records. Agency compliance is subject to the requester's willingness to pay search, copying, and, for commercial requesters, review fees unless waived by the agency. FOIA does not impose any "need-to-know" requirement on requesters, and an agency must disclose any requested information that is not exempted.

1. *Definition of Agency*

FOIA applies to any "agency," which includes any executive department, military department, government corporation, government-controlled corporation, or other establishment in the executive branch of the government, including any independent regulatory agency. The definition includes the Executive Office of the President, but courts have held that components of the Executive Office of the President whose sole function is to advise and assist the president and that do not wield substantial authority independent of the president are not covered. For example, while the Office of Management and Budget is covered by FOIA, the Council of Economic Advisors and the Office of Administration are not. FOIA's definition of *agency* extends to entities that "perform governmental functions and control information of interest to the public" and includes entities that may not be considered agencies under the APA. Important factors in determining whether an entity is an agency subject to FOIA include whether the entity "has any authority in law to make decisions," whether it has substantial independent authority in the exercise of its functions, and whether it deals directly with those subject to its decisions.

2. *Application to Agency Records*

FOIA applies only to "agency records." Agency records are documents that (1) are either created or obtained by an agency and (2) are in that agency's physical possession and under its control, or maintained by an entity under a records-management contract with an agency, at the time of the FOIA request. Generally, records not meeting those two criteria, such as documents held by government contractors, are not agency records, even if they are subject to an agency right of access. However, a nonprofit grantee's research data underlying published research findings produced under a grant and used in developing an agency action that has the force and effect of law are subject to FOIA. Some documents created and maintained by an agency employee, such as desk calendars, electronic calendars, and telephone logs, may be "personal papers" that do not qualify as agency records. FOIA does not compel government agencies to create records. In very rare circumstances, courts may require agencies to attempt to recreate destroyed records or to provide an explanation for records containing codes or notations that mask the meaning of the records. "Records" include information maintained in any format, including an electronic format. However, the creation and use of a computer program to retrieve information stored digitally does not constitute creation of a new record.

3.   *Specificity and Form of Request*

Requesters must "reasonably describe" records sought so as to "enable[] a professional employee of the agency who was familiar with the subject area of the request to locate the records with a reasonable amount of effort." Requesters must also comply with all published rules of the agency.

4.   *Fees and Fee Waivers*

Subject to some limitations, agencies may charge fees, according to published fee schedules, for searching, reviewing, and copying the requested agency records. If a noncommercial requester makes the request, fees may be charged only for search time and copying, and such charges may not be assessed for the first 100 pages of document copying or for the first two hours of search time. If the request is made by an educational or noncommercial scientific institution or a representative of the news media, fees may normally be charged only for search time. Agencies may reduce or waive fees where the disclosure of information is likely to contribute significantly to public understanding of the government activities and is not primarily in the commercial interest of the requester. In the absence of "unusual or exceptional circumstances" related to processing a request, an agency cannot assess search fees (or duplication fees to noncommercial requesters) if it fails to comply with statutory time limits for processing the request.

5.   *Time for Administrative Determination; Administrative Expedition*

An agency is ordinarily required to make its initial determination within twenty working days of a receipt of a request for information, and to make a determination on any appeal within twenty working days of receipt of the appeal. In "unusual circumstances," an agency can extend these deadlines by an additional ten working days. A requester can obtain expedited processing of a request upon a showing of "compelling need" or in other cases determined by the agency to be appropriate. A compelling need exists if failure to obtain the information on an expedited basis could reasonably be expected to pose an imminent threat to the life or physical safety of an individual. In addition, a compelling need exists if "a person primarily engaged in the dissemination of information," such as a journalist or a public-interest group, can show that there is an urgency to inform the public concerning actual or alleged federal government activity. An agency must act on a request for expedition within ten days of its receipt. Where an agency fails to comply with the statutory deadlines, the requester may treat the delay as a denial and either appeal administratively or litigate in federal court.

6.   *Search Required*

Agencies must make reasonable efforts to conduct a search for requested records. The agency cannot limit its search to only certain places if additional sources are likely to turn up the information requested. The agency's search must be "reasonably calculated to recover all relevant documents." However, searches need not be perfect and thus agencies need not prove that they located every responsive record. An agency must pursue leads in found documents that may lead to other responsive documents, and a search may be inadequate if an agency fails to expand the scope of its search upon discovering information suggesting the existence of documents that it has not yet located.

If a requester challenges the adequacy or thoroughness of an agency's search for records in district court, the agency bears the burden of proving the reasonableness of its efforts and must provide details of the procedures used in its search.

7.   *Segregation Requirement*

Where a requested record contains both exempt and nonexempt information, an agency must disclose nonexempt, reasonably segregable portions of the record and indicate the amount of information deleted and the exemption under which the deletion is made. Determinations of whether record portions are reasonably segregable are based on the intelligibility of the nonexempt material and the burden of editing or segregating it.

8.   *Explanation Required*

Where an agency denies a request in whole or in part, the agency must provide the requester with an indication of which information will not be released, a statement of the reasons for withholding the records, a notice of the requester's right of appeal to the head of the agency, and a statement of the names and titles or positions of each person responsible for the denial.

9.   *Format*

FOIA requesters are generally entitled to receive agency records in the format they prefer, except when the effort to do so "would significantly interfere with the operation of the agency's automated information system."

10.   *Administrative Appeal*

A requester may appeal to the head of the agency a denial of a request, an inadequate agency search for records, an agency failure to respond to a request within the statutory time limits, the imposition of excessive fees, or the agency's denial of a request for waiver or reduction of fees. A requester may obtain expedited review upon a showing of "exceptional need or urgency."

11. *Judicial Review*

A requester may seek judicial review of each of the agency actions mentioned in the preceding paragraphs. See § II.

C.   Exemptions

FOIA requires that all government records must be published or made available to the public unless they fall into one of the nine enumerated exemptions in § 552(b). The exemptions are not mandatory bars to disclosure, and therefore an agency—unless otherwise prohibited by a more specific statute—may exercise its discretion to disclose exempted information.

1. Exemption 1 covers documents that are "specifically authorized under criteria established by an Executive Order to be kept secret in the interest of national defense or foreign policy and are in fact properly classified pursuant to such Executive Order."
The classification system is set out in the Information Security Oversight Office (ISOO) of the National Archives and Records Administration pursuant to Executive Order 13,526. The ISOO provisions, set forth in 32 C.F.R. parts 2001 and 2003, provide that information shall be considered for classification only where it concerns (a) military plans, weapons systems, or operations; (b) foreign-government information; (c) intelligence activities (including special activities), intelligence sources or methods, or cryptology; (d) foreign relations or foreign activities of the United States, including confidential sources; (e) scientific, technological, or economic matters relating to the national security; (f) United States Government programs for safeguarding nuclear materials

or facilities; (g) vulnerabilities or capabilities of systems, installations, projects, or plans relating to the national security; or (h) the development, production, or use of weapons of mass destruction. The ISOO provisions prohibit classifying information to conceal violations of law, inefficiency, or administrative error; to prevent embarrassment to a person or organization, or the agency; to restrain competition; to prevent or delay the disclosure of information that does not warrant national security protection; or to thwart public access to basic scientific research not clearly related to the national security.

Courts afford substantial weight to an agency's affidavit concerning information classified under Exemption 1, and an agency is entitled to summary judgment if its affidavits "describe the withheld information and the justification for withholding with reasonable specificity, demonstrating a logical connection between the information and the claimed exemption" and the affidavits "are not controverted by either contrary evidence in the record nor by evidence of bad faith." National security agencies may also refuse to confirm or deny the existence or nonexistence of requested information (a "Glomar" response) whenever the information's existence or nonexistence is also classified.

Courts may conduct *in camera* review of information withheld under Exemption 1. Such review is not automatic, and the courts consider a number of factors, including the likelihood that sensitive information might be inadvertently disclosed, in deciding whether to undertake such review. An agency may also make an *in camera* submission to support its classification decision, but the agency must make its reasons for doing so clear and make as much of the submission as possible available to the party seeking disclosure.

2. Exemption 2 protects from disclosure information "related solely to the internal personnel rules and practices of an agency." Records may be withheld under Exemption 2 only if they relate solely to personnel matters that are routine or trivial and not the sort of material in which the public could reasonably be expected

to have an interest—matters relating to pay, pensions, vacations, hours of work, lunch hours, and parking are examples. Some internal personnel records—for example, case summaries of honor and ethics code hearings concerning cadets at the military academies—have been found to have substantial potential for public interest outside the government and thus not to qualify for Exemption 2. The exemption does not protect documents concerning an agency's internal rules and practices for its personnel to follow in the discharge of their governmental functions. Nor does it protect internal management documents that do not relate to personnel matters. Exempt records must also be "internal" in the sense that the agency ordinarily keeps them to itself for its own use. Administrative markings on agency personnel files—such as file numbers, initials, signatures, routing marks, computer codes, access numbers, storage, location, retrieval markings, and the like—are exempt.

Case law recognizing a "high-2" exemption allowing agencies to withhold materials that could facilitate circumvention of agency regulations or statutes, i.e., material such as operating rules, guidelines, and manuals of procedure for government investigators or examiners, has been repudiated by the U.S. Supreme Court and is no longer good law. However, other exemptions protect from disclosure records that could enable circumvention of agency regulations or statutes.

3. Exemption 3 protects information specifically exempted from disclosure by statute, provided that such statute (a) requires that the matters be withheld from the public in such a manner as to leave no discretion on the issue or (b) establishes particular criteria for withholding or refers to particular types of matters to be withheld and (c) if enacted after March 17, 2009, explicitly cites to the provisions of Exemption 3. The courts have split on whether to afford deference to an agency's interpretation of a statute that purportedly authorizes nondisclosure.

4. Exemption 4 applies to "trade secrets" and to "commercial or financial information obtained from a person and privileged or confidential."

For purposes of Exemption 4, a trade secret includes an "unpatented, secret, commercially valuable plan, appliance, formula, or process, which is used for the making, preparing, compounding, treating, or processing of articles or materials which are trade commodities." A trade secret may also encompass a broader category of information, including any formula, pattern, device, or compilation of information that is used in one's business and that gives him an opportunity to obtain an advantage over competitors who do not know or use it.

Virtually any information tied to commerce or business could qualify as "commercial or financial information" protected under Exemption 4 so long as the information has been generated by a person outside the government and is privileged or confidential. Privileged information includes information that is covered by evidentiary privileges such as the attorney-client privilege. Where information is required to be submitted to the government, the information is considered confidential if it is of the sort not customarily released, and if the disclosure of the information is likely either to impair the government's ability to obtain necessary information in the future or to cause substantial harm to the competitive position of the person from whom the information was obtained. To prove likelihood of competitive harm, the party arguing against disclosure does not have to show actual competitive harm, but it must demonstrate that the information is of a character that is not usually made available to competitors, and that disclosure presents a reasonable likelihood of substantial competitive harm.

Where commercial or financial information is voluntarily submitted to the government, it may be considered confidential if it would be kept "customarily confidential" by the submitter.

Agencies must provide notice to submitters of confidential commercial information in advance of disclosure pursuant to executive order. (See § III.)

5. Exemption 5 shields from mandatory disclosure "inter-agency or intra-agency memorandums or letters which would not be available by law to a party other than an agency in litigation with the agency." The exemption has two basic purposes: (1) to promote full, frank, and candid policymaking debate within and among agencies and (2) to prevent premature disclosure of developing agency actions and policies.

To qualify for protection, a document must satisfy two conditions: its source must be a federal agency, and it must fall within a privilege against discovery under judicial standards that would govern in litigation against the agency that holds it. With respect to the first condition, the source of the document may be an outside consultant hired by the agency who occupies the same position in the decisionmaking process as a government employee (i.e., the "consultants exception"). It does not protect communications to or from an interested person or group seeking a government benefit at the expense of other applicants, even if the group is a quasi-governmental body, such as an Indian tribe, to which the agency has trust obligations. It is not clear whether Exemption 5 can be invoked when the source of the document is a state government or a foreign government.

With respect to the second condition, the exemption includes all government litigation privileges, including the presidential communications privilege (i.e., "executive privilege"), the deliberative process privilege, and other traditional privileges such as attorney-client and work product. In applying the deliberative-process privilege, a general distinction is made between deliberative and predecisional materials, which are afforded protection, and factual and postdecisional materials, which are not. Predecisional, deliberative documents lose their protection if adopted or incorporated by reference in the agency's final decision. Also protected under Exemption 5 are confidential commercial information relating to national monetary policy, factual statements made to government aircraft safety investigators under an assurance of confidentiality, and reports of expert witnesses.

6. Exemption 6 covers "personnel and medical files and similar files the disclosure of which would constitute a clearly unwarranted invasion of personal privacy." Personnel files include files containing personal data such as date and place of birth, parents' names, residences, academic and professional evaluations, and the like. Medical files are files containing assessments or records of an individual's medical or psychological status. The category of "similar files" has "a broad, rather than a narrow, meaning" and includes any record that applies to a particular individual, but not to a corporation.

Exemption 6 applies only where the invasion of personal privacy is real, as opposed to speculative. However, a cognizable privacy invasion exists if disclosure would invite unwarranted intrusion into an individual's privacy, even if the disclosure, by itself, would not cause embarrassment. A privacy interest may exist in information that is "practically obscure" even if the information has, at some point, been made public. Mailing lists and other compilations of names are generally covered by Exemption 6.

The determination of whether a disclosure constitutes a "clearly unwarranted" invasion of privacy requires balancing the privacy interest against the public interest in disclosure, with a tilt in favor of disclosure. The only cognizable "public interest" in disclosure is the disclosure's contribution to the public's understanding of government operations of activities. The Supreme Court has left open the question of whether such a public interest might encompass the potential "derivative uses" of information that would facilitate private monitoring of government activity. To the extent that the requested information reveals that a senior

government official engaged in wrongdoing or misconduct, disclosure is likely in order because the public is entitled to learn
about infractions committed by senior officials.

If information is covered by both Exemption 6 and the Privacy
Act, 5 U.S.C. § 552a, then the Privacy Act forbids agencies from
disclosing that information, and thus the information may not be
disclosed even if a public interest in disclosure can be shown.

7. Exemption 7 protects records or information compiled for law
enforcement purposes to the extent that the production of such
records or information would have one of six specific harms
listed below *(a)–(f)*. An agency must establish a nexus between
the relevant information and law enforcement duties. Courts
may afford deference to the government's claims concerning the
connection with law enforcement duties and may adopt presump-
tions or per se rules that certain categories of records generated
by law enforcement agencies have the necessary nexus. "Law
enforcement" does not include general agency monitoring of its
employees to ensure compliance with applicable requirements.

(a) Exemption 7(A) protects law enforcement records and
information the disclosure of which "could reasonably be
expected to interfere with enforcement proceedings." For
records to qualify under Exemption 7(A), the government
must show that (1) an enforcement proceeding is pending or prospective and (2) release of the information could
reasonably be expected to cause some articulable harm to
that proceeding. Such harms include assisting possible witness intimidation, deterring future witnesses, and allowing
violators to construct defenses that permit violations to go
unchecked. Though Exemption 7(A) requires pending or
prospective law enforcement action, the exemption may
properly be invoked where one case has been closed but further enforcement action may be taken.

(b) Exemption 7(B) applies where disclosure of law enforcement records or information "would deprive a person of

a right to fair trial or an impartial adjudication." To justify
nondisclosure, the government must show "(1) that a trial
or adjudication is pending or truly imminent and (2) that
it is more probable than not that disclosure of the material sought would seriously interfere with the fairness of
those proceedings." Serious interference with the fairness
of proceedings includes publicity that is of such a nature
and degree to compromise judicial fairness, and disclosures
of information not available under discovery rules that
would confer an unfair advantage on one of the parties to a
proceeding.

(c) Exemption 7(C) protects law enforcement records and
information the disclosure of which could reasonably be
expected to constitute an unwarranted invasion of privacy.
Like Exemption 6, Exemption 7(C) requires a balancing of
the public interest in disclosure against the invasion of personal privacy, though the protection of privacy is broader
under Exemption 7(C) than under Exemption 6. Exemption 7(C) may be used to protect the identities of persons
connected to law enforcement activities, including persons
investigated by law enforcement agencies, informants who
do not qualify for protection under Exemption 7(D), FBI
agents, other officers involved in investigations and other
individuals connected to criminal investigations.

For purposes of Exemption 7(C), a third party's request
for law enforcement records or information about a private
citizen can reasonably be expected to invade that citizen's
privacy. Such an invasion of privacy is "unwarranted" if the
request seeks no "official information" about a government
agency but merely records that the government happens to
be storing.

The relevant privacy interest is not limited to information about oneself; release of information about a person
may be an unwarranted invasion of the privacy of that person's family members. For example, family members may

assert a privacy interest in the crime-scene photographs of a deceased family member held by law enforcement officials. The "personal privacy" interests protected by Exemption 7(C) are those of natural persons; thus the exemption may not be invoked to protect the "privacy" of a corporation.

Though a privacy interest may be overcome by showing a sufficiently strong interest in public disclosure, when the asserted public interest in disclosure is government officials' negligent or otherwise improper performance of their duties, the requester must establish more than a bare suspicion of such negligence or misconduct in order to obtain disclosure. Rather, the requester must produce evidence that would warrant a belief by a reasonable person that the alleged government impropriety might have occurred.

(d) Exemption 7(D) protects law enforcement records and information that could reasonably be expected to identify a confidential source, including a state, local, or foreign agency or authority or any private institution that has furnished information on a confidential basis. Exemption 7(D) also covers information furnished by a confidential source or information compiled either by a criminal law enforcement authority in the course of a criminal investigation or by an agency conducting a lawful national security intelligence investigation.

Exemption 7(D) extends to a broad group of information purveyors the most comprehensive protection afforded to law enforcement information by FOIA. All information received from sources during the course of criminal investigations enjoys a "presumption" of confidentiality. Information provided by a source is considered confidential if the source reasonably believed that the information would remain confidential, even if the information is contained in a document that the agency does not usually treat as confidential. The identity of a source is protected whenever the source has provided information under express assurance of confidentiality or under circumstances from which such an assurance could reasonably be inferred.

Exemption 7(D) is not limited in duration. The protections of the exemption are not diminished when the investigation closes, when the prosecution is at an end, or even when the source dies. Where an informant has testified in open court, the government may still invoke the exemption to protect information not disclosed in the informant's testimony.

(e) Exemption 7(E) covers law enforcement records and information that would disclose techniques and procedures for law enforcement investigations or prosecutions, or would disclose guidelines for law enforcement investigations or prosecutions if such disclosure could reasonably be expected to allow violators of the law to circumvent law enforcement and evade detection.

The exemption protects from disclosure techniques and procedures not well known to the public and, in addition, covers even commonly known procedures and techniques where the relevant disclosure might diminish their effectiveness.

(f) Exemption 7(F) protects law enforcement records and information the disclosure of which could reasonably be expected to endanger the life or physical safety of any individual. Unlike Exemption 7(C), Exemption 7(F) contains no balancing requirement.

8. Exemption 8 applies to matters that are "contained in or related to examination, operating, or condition reports prepared by, on behalf of, or for the use of an agency responsible for the regulation or supervision of financial institutions." All records that concern a bank's financial condition and operations and that are in the possession and control of a federal agency responsible for the regulation or supervision of financial institutions are exempt from disclosure.

9. Exemption 9 applies to "geological and geophysical information and data, including maps, concerning wells."

D. Exclusions

Records covered by an exclusion from FOIA are treated "as not subject to the requirements of" the act. When documents requested fall within one of the exclusions, the agency will respond by stating that no records responsive to the request exist. There are three exclusions: Exclusion (c)(1) applies to Exemption 7(A) materials where the investigation involves a possible violation of criminal law and there is reason to believe that (a) the subject of the investigation is unaware that it is ongoing, and (b) disclosure of the records could reasonably be expected to interfere with enforcement efforts. Exclusion (c)(2) applies to requests for information involving the threatened identification of confidential informants in criminal proceedings. Exclusion (c)(3) applies to classified records kept by the FBI relating to foreign intelligence, counterintelligence, and international terrorism.

II. JUDICIAL REVIEW

A. Jurisdiction

U.S. district courts have jurisdiction to enjoin an agency from withholding agency records and to order production of any records improperly withheld. District courts also have jurisdiction to determine whether an agency has charged excessive fees for a FOIA request and whether the agency has improperly denied a fee waiver request. Courts may also have jurisdiction to review agency failure to publish information required by § 552(a)(1) and refusal to make information available for inspection and copying under § 552(a)(2).

B.   Exhaustion of Administrative Remedies

FOIA requesters must exhaust administrative remedies before filing FOIA suits. A requester "shall be deemed to have exhausted his administrative remedies . . . if the agency fails to comply with the applicable time limit provisions." If the agency responds to an initial request after the twenty working days permitted for a response to the request, but before the filing of a lawsuit, the requester is then obligated to pursue an administrative appeal before initiating litigation.

Even if an agency fails to meet the time limits and the requester brings suit, courts may stay the litigation, retain jurisdiction, and allow the agency additional time to process the request if the agency can show that "exceptional circumstances exist and the agency is exercising due diligence in responding to the request." Exceptional circumstances exist only where the agency "is deluged with a volume of requests for information vastly in excess of that anticipated by Congress" and "the existing resources are inadequate to deal with the volume of such requests within the time limits" of the act.

C.   Statute of Limitations

The general federal statute of limitations of six years applies to FOIA suits and begins to run once the requester has, or is deemed to have, exhausted administrative remedies.

D.   Venue

Venue for a FOIA action is in the federal district in which the plaintiff resides or has his principal place of business, or in which the agency records are situated, or in the District of Columbia.

E.   Burden of Proof

The agency always has the burden of proving (1) that the records in question or any parts withheld are exempt from disclosure, and (2) that each document requested either has been produced, is unidentifiable, or is wholly exempt from disclosure.

As a general rule, the agency must assert all exemptions at the same time, in the original district court proceedings. However, a court has allowed assertion of additional exemptions when the failure to assert them initially resulted from a mistake and the failure to allow assertion of the exemption would put the safety or privacy of a third party at risk. The agency may rely in the district court on an exemption it did not raise administratively.

F.   De Novo Review

Agency decisions to withhold information are reviewed de novo by the courts.

G.   *Vaughn* Index

Courts usually require agencies in FOIA litigation to provide the requester with a detailed explanation of the agency's refusal to disclose requested documents. This "*Vaughn* index" must include (1) an itemization and description of the records withheld; (2) a detailed justification for the claim of exemption; and (3) an index cross-referencing the justification with the record or portion thereof to which it applied. Courts have discretion to refuse a requester's motion seeking a *Vaughn* index or to require the submission of the index for *in camera* review.

H.   *In Camera* Inspection

Courts have broad discretionary power to conduct an *in camera* review of disputed information. See, for example, § I.C.1.

I.   Discovery

Discovery is available in FOIA cases, but usually courts severely restrict its scope. Discovery is appropriate to determine the scope of the agency's search for responsive records or to investigate factual questions concerning whether the agency's exemption claim is well founded. Discovery may not be had where the plaintiff is seeking to obtain information contained in the withheld records or to question investigatory activities undertaken by the agency.

J.   Attorney's Fees and Costs

A court may assess against the United States reasonable attorney's fees and other litigation costs reasonably incurred in any FOIA case in which the complainant substantially prevails. The agency must pay such an award directly out of its own budget. In awarding fees and costs, courts generally consider four criteria: (1) the public benefit, if any, from the case; (2) the commercial benefit to the plaintiff; (3) the nature of the plaintiff's interest in the records sought; and (4) the reasonableness of the government's legal position in withholding the records.

To obtain fees, a plaintiff must "substantially prevail" in the litigation. The plaintiff must have "obtained relief," though this need not have been through a judicial order or consent decree; a voluntary or unilateral change in position by the agency suffices. The plaintiff does not need to have won the release of all requested documents, but the litigation must have had a substantially causative effect on the release of information by the agency. Even where no documents are released, however, the requester may be deemed to have "substantially prevailed" if the suit compels an agency to comply with the law.

K.   Sanctions

Sanctions may be imposed against employees of an agency for failing to comply with FOIA. A proceeding for sanctions may be initiated by the U.S. Office of Special Counsel where (1) a court orders production of an agency record improperly withheld; (2) the court assesses reasonable attorney's fees and other litigation costs against the government; and (3) the court issues a written finding that the circumstances surrounding the withholding suggest that agency personnel acted arbitrarily and capriciously.

III. SUITS TO ENJOIN DISCLOSURE ("REVERSE-FOIA" CASES)

A person who has submitted information to the government has a legally cognizable interest in that information and may seek judicial review under the APA of an agency's decision to grant a FOIA request for the information.

While FOIA itself places no constraints on release of information held by government agencies, other laws may constrain agency discretion to make disclosures under FOIA. The party seeking to prevent the disclosure of information bears the burden of justifying nondisclosure.

While FOIA does not require predisclosure notification to submitters, agencies are required by Executive Order 12,600 to issue regulations providing for such notice to submitters of "confidential commercial information" and for receipt of their objections to disclosure.

IV. FEDERAL ADVISORY COMMITTEE ACT

The Federal Advisory Committee Act (FACA), 5 U.S.C. app. II, in general applies to any committee not wholly composed of federal employees established by statute, or established or utilized by the executive branch, for the purpose of providing advice to the president or to one or more agencies or officers of the federal government. The act's requirements do not apply to subcommittees as long as they do not function as or make decisions that bind the full committee.

An advisory committee is "established" for purposes of FACA only if the government itself has "organized" or "formed" the committee. Whether a committee is "utilized" within the meaning of FACA depends on three factors: (a) whether the committee was formed at the federal government's prompting; (b) whether the government

exercised control over the committee's operations or affairs; and
(c) whether the committee received federal funding.

An advisory committee is subject to FACA only where it renders
advice to the president, the Congress, or an executive-branch agency,
including any independent regulatory agency.

FACA requires covered committees to be fairly balanced in terms
of the points of view represented and the functions to be performed,
although courts have not been demanding in their interpretation of this
provision. Before an advisory committee meets or takes action, a charter for it must be filed with (a) the administrator of the General Services
Administration, in the case of presidential advisory committees, or
(b) the agency head to whom the advisory committee reports and the
standing committees of the Senate and the House of Representatives
having legislative jurisdiction over the agency. The charter must set
forth the committee's objectives and scope, the time period necessary
for it to carry out its functions, the agency responsible for providing the committee support, and the duties for which the committee is
responsible.

The public must be given timely notice of committee meetings (at
least fifteen days in advance) through publication of the committee's
agenda in the *Federal Register*. Advisory committee meetings must be
open to the public, unless the president or the head of the agency to
which the advisory committee reports determines that the meeting
may be closed in accordance with the exemptions listed in the Government in the Sunshine Act. Individuals may "attend, appear before, or
file statements" with the committee, subject to reasonable regulations.
Records, reports, transcripts, minutes, agendas, working papers, drafts,
or other documents made available to or prepared by an advisory committee shall be made available to the public, except to the extent that
the material is protected from disclosure under one or more applicable
FOIA exemptions.

Each agency is responsible for providing support services to its
advisory committees, and each advisory committee meeting must be
chaired or attended by a designated government officer. Each committee has a two-year life span unless a different period is specified by

statute or the committee's creating authority takes action to renew its existence. The provisions of FACA may be enforced by a private action under the APA against the agency to which the committee reports, although courts are divided on the scope of relief available.

FACA also requires that agencies make available to any person, at actual cost of duplication, copies of transcripts of agency proceedings or advisory committee meetings.

V.   GOVERNMENT IN THE SUNSHINE ACT

The Government in the Sunshine Act, codified primarily at 5 U.S.C. § 552b, applies to any agency subject to FOIA and headed by a collegial body of two or more individual members, a majority of whom are appointed by the president with the advice and consent of the Senate, and to any subdivision of such an agency authorized to act on its behalf.

An agency subject to the Sunshine Act must give reasonable notice of its meetings and make every portion of its meetings open to public observation, unless the agency has properly decided to close the meeting, or a portion thereof, pursuant to one of the act's ten exemptions. The act does not give the public a right to participate at meetings. Moreover, the act does not preclude collegial bodies from deciding matters without holding meetings, such as by members placing notations indicating concurrence or dissent on a packet of material laying out the issues and proposed resolution.

The act's exemptions permitting closure of meetings generally mirror those in FOIA, with two notable exceptions: internal privileged communications that would not prematurely disclose proposed agency actions (FOIA Exemption 5) are not included, while discussions of most agency adjudicatory matters are. An agency may not close any portion of a meeting without a majority of the members voting to close that portion of the meeting. The agency has the burden of proving that the decision to close a meeting was lawful.

For purposes of the act, the term "meeting" means the deliberations of at least the number of individuals required to take action on
behalf of the agency where such deliberations determine or result in
the joint conduct or disposition of official agency business, except that
discussions of administrative matters, such as scheduling a future
meeting, do not constitute meetings. Thus, a gathering of a subset of
board members that does not constitute a quorum of the board is not
a covered meeting. In addition, a meeting even of a quorum is not
a "meeting" subject to the open meeting requirement if it is not "sufficiently focused on discrete proposals or issues as to cause or to be
likely to cause the individual participating members to form reasonably firm positions regarding matters pending or likely to arise before
the agency." Meetings include not only sessions in which members of
the body are physically present in the same location, but also sessions
in which members interact contemporaneously by telephone or other
technological means. It is not clear whether the act covers noncontem-
poraneous digital or electronic interactions between members, such as
by way of e-mail.

The act provides district courts with subject matter jurisdiction
to enforce the requirements of the act relating to open meetings and
records by declaratory judgment, injunctive relief, or other appropriate
relief. Invalidation of the agency action is not a proper remedy under
the act, but requiring a meeting to be open or records to be disclosed is.
A prevailing party is entitled to reasonable attorney's fees and other litigation costs.

PART SIX

GOVERNMENT MANAGEMENT OF THE ADMINISTRATIVE PROCESS

PART SIX
GOVERNMENT MANAGEMENT OF
THE ADMINISTRATIVE PROCESS

I.   SCOPE

This section concerns procedures relating to the management of administrative functions across federal agencies, particularly requirements for agencies to submit proposed actions for advance review and opportunities for executive and congressional supervision or correction of agency decisionmaking.

II.   CONGRESSIONAL MANAGEMENT
OF AGENCY ACTION

The Constitution prohibits members or houses of Congress, or Congress itself, from being, appointing, or removing officers of the United States, or from vetoing an agency action other than through the enactment of legislation. Therefore, Congress has no power of direct supervision or management over agencies even though its power to define and limit an agency's authority is virtually plenary within the bounds of the Constitution.

Nevertheless, Congress has the recognized constitutional authority to oversee agency action for a number of purposes, especially for determining whether new legislation is necessary or appropriate. Congress's ultimate control over the agency's budget and its organic statute means that congressional views will have influence with the agency. Also, inherent in the legislative power is a power of inquiry, including the power to subpoena witnesses and documents (subject to applicable privileges, including an executive privilege of uncertain scope) and to enforce compliance therewith through the contempt power. Congressional investigation and public hearings can lead to public scrutiny and political pressure on the agency.

Attempts by members or committees of Congress to influence the outcome of an agency proceeding are subject to the APA's constraints on ex parte communications and other restrictions that apply to such attempts by private persons. Beyond those requirements, however, congressional attempts to influence agency proceedings are largely unregulated. Use of the congressional hearing power to try to influence the outcome of a pending formal adjudication has been held a violation of due process, although hearings to explore policy issues that might be involved in an adjudication can be permissible and appropriate if properly managed. Outside the context of formal or other on-the-record proceedings, a court is not likely to set aside an agency decision because of alleged congressional influence unless the evidence shows that the pressure brought to bear caused the agency action to be affected by factors that are not relevant under the governing statute.

Under the Congressional Review Act, 5 U.S.C. §§ 801–808, a rule cannot take effect if Congress passes a joint resolution disapproving the rule. The act exempts rules relating to agency management or personnel or agency organization, procedure, or practice, as well as rules of particular applicability. Before a rule can take effect, the promulgating agency must submit a copy of the rule and a concise general statement relating thereto to both houses of Congress and the comptroller general. A joint resolution of disapproval must be introduced within sixty days of such submission and is considered according to expedited procedures set out in the act. A *major* rule *cannot* take effect for sixty days after it has been submitted to Congress, a delay designed to ensure Congress has time to disapprove the rule. Major rules include any rule (other than one promulgated under the Telecommunications Act of 1996 and its amendments) that the administrator of the Office of Management and Budget's Office of Information and Regulatory Affairs (OIRA) finds will result in an annual effect on the economy of $100 million or more; a major increase in costs or prices; or significant adverse effects on competition, employment, investment, productivity, or the ability of U.S.–based enterprises to compete with foreign enterprises.

III. PRESIDENTIAL MANAGEMENT OF AGENCY ACTION

A.   President's Constitutional Authority

Two provisions of Article II of the Constitution are conceived to be the primary sources of the president's authority to manage agency action. The first, known as the Vesting Clause, states that the "executive power" shall be vested in the president. U.S. Const., Art. II, Sec. 1, cl. 1. The second, known as the "Take Care Clause," states that the president "shall take care that the laws be faithfully executed." U.S. Const., Art. II, Sec. 3. In addition, the president may "require the opinion, in writing, of the principal officer in each of the executive departments, upon any subject relating to the duties of their respective offices." U.S. Const., Art. II, Sec. 2, cl. 1. These provisions furnish authority to the president to supervise, consult with, and obtain information from executive officers in the performance of their statutory duties. For these purposes, an executive department includes cabinet departments, independent executive agencies, and independent regulatory commissions.

However, most statutes place rulemaking and adjudicatory authority in the agency head or the agency itself, not in the president. The extent to which the president can order agency officials to take actions within the officials' delegated authority is uncertain.

In practice, the president's exercise of his supervisory power has largely correlated with his ability on the one hand to appoint, with the advice and consent of the Senate, principal officers, U.S. Const., Art. II, Sec. 2, cl. 2, and on the other hand to remove agency officials who ignore his direction. While the Constitution may be read to preclude any statutory limitation on the president's appointment power, it is not uncommon for a statute creating an agency to place some limits on whom the president may appoint to head the agency. No cases have addressed the constitutionality of such limits, but presidents since Ronald Reagan have issued signing statements to the effect that some such limitations are an unconstitutional restriction on the president's appointment powers.

The Constitution, other than in the impeachment clause, does not address who may remove executive officers or on what basis, but impeachment is by no means the only permissible route to removal of executive officers. Where statutes do not address removal of particular officers, it is presumed that the president may remove them at will, except perhaps when their sole function is the adjudication of administrative cases. Thus, under these circumstances, the president may remove an official simply for failure to follow supervision.

A number of statutes provide that an officer may be removed only for cause. Exactly what kind of conduct can constitute "cause" is unclear, but in practice removals on this basis are rare, and the Court has never directly addressed the issue. However, in a case involving the ability of Congress to remove the comptroller general for "inefficiency," "neglect of duty," and "malfeasance," it characterized these terms as very broad and said they could be interpreted to include "any number of actual or perceived transgressions of the legislative will."

The validity of "for-cause" removal provisions is not well defined by case law. Even with respect to purely executive officers, such a provision may be valid if it does not impede the president's ability to perform his constitutional duties. This does not necessarily mean, however, that Congress could constrain the president's ability to remove a principal officer, such as the secretary of state, whose job involves execution of authorities granted by the Constitution to the president. Moreover, in some circumstances, "dual for-cause" provisions (whereby a principal officer can be removed only for cause and an inferior officer can be removed only for cause by that principal officer) unconstitutionally constrain the president's ability to oversee the executive branch.

B. Regulatory Review

Although the specifics have varied with each administration, all presidents since Richard Nixon have issued executive orders that require executive agencies, but not independent regulatory commissions, to perform certain analyses and submit proposed and final rules to an office in the Executive Office of the President for its review before publication. Since President Reagan's E.O. 12,291 (1981), responsibility for such review has been lodged with OIRA. The procedural requirements of such review are set out above in Part Two, § IV.

The relevant executive orders have also included provisions concerning regulatory planning, including the semiannual publication of a Unified Regulatory Agenda, identifying and describing all regulations each agency has under development or review. Under the most recent of these, President Clinton's E.O. 12,866, agencies must prepare an annual Regulatory Plan, submitted to OIRA and included in the Unified Regulatory Agenda, describing and justifying the most important significant regulatory actions that the agency reasonably expects to issue in proposed or final form in that fiscal year or thereafter. Under E.O. 12,866, but not under its predecessors, these planning requirements extend to independent regulatory commissions as well as executive agencies.

Current executive orders, which are by definition subject to rescission or revision by successor administrations, also require or encourage the pursuit of specific substantive policies by requiring agencies to (a) prepare a cost-benefit analysis for significant regulatory actions; (b) pursue the most cost-effective regulatory alternative; (c) consider the impacts of proposed regulations on certain specified interests, such as federalism, the environmental health and safety of children, Indian tribal governments, and takings of private property; and (d) undertake periodic review of existing rules.

Most executive orders governing agency rulemaking provide, as they must under the Constitution, that their provisions apply only "to the extent permitted by law." A violation of their requirements does not affect the validity of the rule or provide a basis for judicial review. Enforcement of the provisions of the oversight orders is left to the political process.

IV. STATUTORY REQUIREMENTS

A.   Paperwork Reduction Act

The Paperwork Reduction Act of 1980, which covers essentially all agencies (including independent regulatory commissions and the Executive Office of the President) except the Government Accountability Office (GAO) and the Federal Election Commission, applies to agency "collection of information." This term includes an agency's (1) collecting facts or information from ten or more persons, (2) requiring ten or more persons to disclose facts or opinions to the public or third parties, (3) requiring ten or more persons to maintain records, (4) collecting information from federal agencies or employees for statistical purposes. It does not include the collection of information as part of criminal investigations, civil or administrative proceedings to which the government is a party, or intelligence activities.

Before an agency may engage in the collection of information, it must

(1)   undertake an internal review to evaluate the need for the information, describe the information to be collected, create a plan for its collection, and estimate the burden on private parties that the collection will impose;

(2)   publicly announce its reasons for collecting the information, the way in which the information will be used, the burden its collection will impose, whether responses are voluntary or mandatory, and the fact that in the absence of a valid control number a person is not bound to respond to any collection requirement;

(3)   submit the proposal for public notice and comment;

(4)   submit the proposal and an accompanying justification to OIRA, which then seeks public comment on the agency's submission for thirty days.

If OIRA takes no action within sixty days, the proposed collection of information is deemed approved. In the case of a collection of information that is not part of or required by a rule that goes through notice and comment, OIRA may disapprove the collection if it determines that it is "unnecessary for any reason." In the case of a collection of information that is part of or required by a rule that goes through notice and comment, OIRA must submit comments as part of that proceeding and may disapprove the collection of information only if the agency's response to OIRA's comments was unreasonable. An independent regulatory commission may override an OIRA disapproval by majority vote. The Paperwork Reduction Act states that OIRA's approval of (or failure to act on) a proposed collection of information is not subject to judicial review, but it is silent about judicial review of disapprovals. Presumably, persons adversely affected by a disapproval can obtain judicial review under the APA, subject to standard requirements for judicial review, and there is some authority permitting review.

When OIRA approves a collection of information, it assigns a control number to the collection. No one is subject to any penalty for failing to comply with an agency's collection of information requirement that does not display a valid control number. The absence of a valid control number, however, is no defense to a penalty for filing false information or for failing to file information required to be filed by statute.

B.   Government Performance and Results Act

The Government Performance and Results Act of 1993, as amended by the GPRA Modernization Act of 2010, requires agencies to prepare a strategic plan and a performance plan annually, and to post these plans on the agency's website and notify the president and Congress of their availability.

The strategic plan must include a mission statement, a general statement of goals, a description of how those goals are to be achieved, a description of obstacles to their achievement, and a description of how the agency's performance goals contribute to its strategic goals, among other statements. The performance plan must establish performance goals, express those goals in objective, quantifiable, and measurable form (unless the director of OMB determines it is not feasible to do so), describe how these goals contribute to the agency's strategic plan and the federal government's performance goals, identify how these goals are to be achieved, provide a basis for measuring its performance, and identify low-priority activities, among other statements.

The agency head must also make available updates on performance, comparing actual performance achievements with the agency's performance goals, not less than 150 days after the end of the fiscal year, and more frequently if it can do so at a reasonable level of administrative burden. These updates must provide a detailed review and assessment of the agency's successes and failures in achieving its performance goals. OMB must make an annual determination of whether the agency met its performance goals, and report on unmet goals to the head of the agency, the House Committee on Oversight and Governmental Reform, and the GAO. If the agency's activities have not met its performance goals as determined by OMB for one fiscal year, the agency must designate a senior official to oversee its performance improvement and must submit a performance improvement plan to OMB. If OMB determines the agency's activities have not met its performance goals for two consecutive years, the agency head must submit to Congress a description of the actions the administration will take to improve performance, and describe any additional funding the agency will obligate to achieve the goal. If OMB determines the agency has not met its performance goals for three consecutive fiscal years, OMB shall submit recommendations to Congress on actions to improve the agency's performance, including reauthorization proposals, statutory changes, and planned executive actions.

The director of OMB must coordinate with agencies to improve the performance of the federal government and to establish priority goals, and every two years, or as otherwise determined by the director of OMB, the head of each agency shall identify a set of priority goals.

C. Regulatory Flexibility Act

The Regulatory Flexibility Act of 1980, 5 U.S.C. §§ 601–612, requires agencies to consider the special needs and concerns of small entities in the regulatory process. Small entities include small businesses as defined in the Small Business Act, 15 U.S.C. §§ 631, et seq.; not-for-profit organizations that are not dominant in their field; and governmental jurisdictions with a population of less than 50,000.

1. *Unified Agenda*

In October and April of each year, each agency must publish a "regulatory flexibility agenda" in the *Federal Register* that identifies and describes all rules under consideration that are likely to have a significant economic impact on a substantial number of small entities. The agenda must be submitted to the chief counsel for advocacy of the Small Business Administration (SBA) for comment.

2. *Regulatory Flexibility Analysis*

When proposing a regulation subject to notice-and-comment requirements, whether under the APA or any other law, an agency must make available for public comment an initial regulatory flexibility analysis (IRFA), unless the agency head certifies that the proposed rule will not have a significant economic impact on a substantial number of small entities. Courts have interpreted the significant economic impact as being limited to the direct cost effects of having to comply with a regulation and not including the indirect economic effects on small entities that may result from a regulation. The IRFA must be submitted to the chief counsel for advocacy of the SBA, and either a copy of the IRFA or a summary must be published in the *Federal Register*. An IRFA must contain a description of the reasons why the agency is considering the rule, a statement of the objectives of and legal basis for the rule, a description of and (where feasible) an estimate of the number of small entities to which the rule will apply, a description of any reporting or record-keeping requirements contained in the rule, an identification of other federal rules that may duplicate or overlap with the rule, and a description of significant alternatives to the rule that would accomplish the stated objectives while minimizing economic effects on small entities. The Consumer Financial Protection Bureau must also include a discussion of those alternatives, a description of any increase in the cost of credit for small entities resulting from the proposed rule, a description of alternatives to the proposed rule that accomplish the stated objections of applicable statutes and minimize any increase in the cost of credit for small entities, and advice for small entities regarding impacts of the proposed rule on the cost of credit.

In the case of rules issued by the Environmental Protection Agency, the Consumer Financial Protection Bureau, or the Occupational Safety and Health Administration, the agency must, prior to publication of the IRFA, notify the chief counsel for advocacy of the potential impacts of the proposed rule on small entities, so that he may identify representatives of the likely affected small entities for their advice and recommendations about the potential impacts. Unless this requirement is waived by the chief counsel for advocacy, these agencies must then convene a review panel consisting of employees from the agency, OIRA, and the chief counsel's office to review the proposed regulation, any other material developed in connection with the proposed rule, and the comments of the small-entity representatives. Within sixty days, the review panel must publicly report on the comments and its findings on the issues discussed in the IRFA. Other agencies *may* in their discretion also utilize this procedure if they wish.

Unless the agency head certifies that the final rule will not have a significant economic impact on a substantial number of small entities, it must be published with a final regulatory flexibility analysis (FRFA). The FRFA must contain a statement of the need for and objectives of the rule; a statement of and response to significant issues raised by the comments received (including in particular those of the chief counsel for advocacy of the SBA); a description of the small entities to which the rule will apply and an estimate of their number; a description of any reporting or record-keeping requirements; a description of the steps the agency has taken to minimize the economic impact on small entities, including a statement of the reasons for adopting the alternative selected and for not adopting other alternatives, and, in the case of the Consumer Financial Protection Bureau, a description of steps the agency has taken to minimize any additional cost of credit for small entities. If a rule is a response to an emergency, the head of an agency may delay the completion of the FRFA until not later than 180 days after the publication of the final rule. If the FRFA is not published within 180 days, the rule automatically lapses and has no effect.

Neither the chief counsel nor a Regulatory Review Panel has authority to veto or reject an agency proposal or regulatory flexibility analysis. The chief counsel is required to report annually to the president and to relevant congressional committees on agency compliance with the act and is authorized to appear as amicus curiae in any action seeking judicial review of a rule.

3. *Periodic Review of Rules*

The Regulatory Flexibility Act also requires agencies to engage in a ten-year review cycle of their regulations that have a significant economic effect on a substantial number of small entities. Each year agencies are to publish in the *Federal Register* the list of such rules that are to be reviewed in the following twelve months.

4. *Judicial Review*

A small entity adversely affected or aggrieved by final agency action may obtain judicial review under the APA of an agency's compliance with the requirements applicable to FRFAs, the validity of any certification that a rule will not have a significant economic effect on a substantial number of small entities, and an agency's compliance with the requirement for periodic review of its rules. The act establishes a maximum statute of limitations for such actions at one year from the date of the final agency action. The act allows a court, in addition to or in lieu of its other remedial powers under the APA, to defer the enforcement of a rule against small entities.

D. Attorney General Supervision of Litigation

By statute, the Department of Justice authorizes and handles most litigation involving agencies, including both enforcement actions that an agency wishes to bring and challenges to agency action under the APA. Even where an agency does have independent litigating authority, the attorney general and the solicitor general, with rare exceptions, have the exclusive authority to pursue and conduct litigation in the Supreme Court on behalf of the agency. By controlling the agency's litigation, the Department of Justice is able to affect the manner in which agencies perform their statutory duties.

INDEX